Easy Grammar Grade 3
Student Workbook

Wanda C. Phillips

Easy Grammar Systems

SCOTTSDALE, ARIZONA 85255

Printed in the United States

© 2006

PREPOSITIONS

above	from
across	in
after	inside
around	into
at	of
before	off
behind	on
below	out
beside	over
between	through
by	to
down	under
during	up
for	with

Name_____   **PREPOSITIONS**

Date_____

A.   Rhyming: Words that rhyme have the same sound at the end.

Examples: top / pop   red / head

1.   Write a preposition that rhymes with *clown*.   _____

2.   Write a preposition that rhymes with *clover*.   _____

3.   Write a preposition that rhymes with *thunder*.   _____

4.   Write a preposition that rhymes with *drum*.   _____

5.   Write six words that rhyme with the preposition, *at*.

_____   _____

_____   _____

_____   _____

B.   Our language is interesting. We use definite words to be more exact.

Example: *To look* means to set eyes on something in order to see.

If we want to be more specific, we can use words like *glance* or *stare*.

To glance means to look at something for a very short time.
To stare means to look at something for a long time.

Use three of your rhyming words for *at* to complete each sentence.

1.   I looked at the _____.

2.   I glanced at the _____.

3.   I stared at the _____.

2

Name_____ **PREPOSITIONS**

Date_____

A. Write the prepositions that have only two letters.

a _   b _   i _   o _

o _   t _   u _

B. Write the prepositions that have three letters.

f _ _   o _ _   o _ _

C. Write the following prepositions in alphabetical order.

Remember: **Look at the first letter. Find the boldfaced letter that comes first in the alphabet. Write that word on the first line. Find the letter that comes next in the alphabet. Write that word second. Use this method to write your list.**

through   inside   during   with

_____

_____

_____

_____

Name_____   **PREPOSITIONS**

Date_____

A. Write the prepositions that begin with *be.*

    b e _ _ _   b e _ _ _ _   b e _ _ _ _ _

    b e _ _ _ _   b e _ _ _ _ _ _

    Which preposition begins with *b* but not with *be?* _____

B. Two prepositions end with *side.* Write those prepositions.

    _____

    _____

C. Write these prepositions that begin with *a* in alphabetical order.

**Remember: When the first letter is the same, you look at the
               second letter.**

       after   across   above   at   around

1. _____

2. _____

3. _____

4. _____

5. _____
4

Name_____   **PREPOSITIONS**

Date_____

A. Look at the picture. Then, fill in the blank with a preposition that fits.

   1.

      The sun is _____ the hill.

   2.

      The sun is _____ the hill.

B. Draw a picture and write a sentence:

   1. Draw a hill. Then, draw something **beside** the hill.

      Write a sentence to tell what is **beside** the hill.

   _____

   2. Draw a hill. Then, draw something going **down** the hill.

      Write a sentence to tell what is going **down** the hill.

   _____

Name_____   **PREPOSITIONS**

Date_____

A. Rhyming: Write nine words that rhyme with the preposition, *by*.

Remember: Words that rhyme end in the same sound.

_____   _____   _____

_____   _____   _____

_____   _____   _____

B. Homonyms: Homonyms are words that sound the same but have
                           different meanings.

                Example: tea / tee
                           Tea is a drink. *Tee* is the item on which a golf ball is
                           placed. *Tea* and *tee* are both pronounced *tē*.

Write a preposition for the following homonyms:

1. four - _____   3. inn - _____

2. two - _____   4. threw - _____

C. Draw a tree.   Draw something **in** the tree.

        Write a sentence to tell what is **in** the tree.

_____

6

A. Write the following prepositions in alphabetical order.

Remember: Look at the first letter. Find the boldfaced letter that comes first in the alphabet. Write that word on the first line. Find the letter that comes next in the alphabet. Write that word second. Use this method to write your list.

under   **b**etween   **i**nto   **a**round   **o**ff   **d**uring

1. _____   4. _____

2. _____   5. _____

3. _____   6. _____

B. Draw a hill. Draw something going up the hill.

Write a sentence to tell what is going **up** the hill.

_____

C. Write the prepositions that contain six or more letters:

1. i_____   3. a_____   5. b_____   7. b_____

2. b_____   4. a_____   6. b_____   8. t_____

7

		FREE		

8

PREPOSITIONAL PHRASES

A **phrase** is a group of words.

two words:	for you
three words:	out the door
four words:	in a candy store
five or more words:	with my mom and dad

A **prepositional phrase** starts with a preposition and ends with a noun or pronoun. To make it easy, let's say that a prepositional phrase usually ends with something you can see.

Examples: **on** the **table**

behind a **chair**

with Tom

Sometimes, **describing words** are included in a prepositional phrase.

Examples: **on** the kitchen **table**

behind a red **chair**

A. Directions: Write words to complete each prepositional phrase.

1. down _____

2. under _____

3. across _____

4. with _____

5. in _____

6. to _____

🐢 🐢 🐢 🐢 🐢 🐢 🐢 🐢 🐢 🐢 🐢 🐢 🐢 🐢 🐢 🐢 🐢 🐢

B. Directions: Unscramble the following prepositional phrases:

1. picnic on a - _____

2. old inside an shed - _____

3. tunnel the through - _____

4. by car that yellow - _____

5. the diving off board - _____

6. a baseball after game - _____

7. water into cold the - _____

10

Name_____

Date_____

Directions: Fill in the blank with a word (or words) that makes sense. Then,
write the prepositional phrase on the line.

Example: Rod walked **around** a ____lake_____.

prepositional phrase: __around a lake__

1. Our cat is lying **by** the _____.

prepositional phrase: _____

2. They stopped **at** a _____.

prepositional phrase: _____

3. **Before** _____, we played a game.

prepositional phrase: _____

4. This box is made **of** _____.

prepositional phrase: _____

5. Jane ran **for** the _____.

prepositional phrase: _____

6. **During** a _____, Mom served cake.

prepositional phrase: _____

7. We rode **on** a _____.

prepositional phrase: _____11

A. Directions: Fill in the blank with a word (or words) that makes sense.
                 Then, write the prepositional phrase on the line.

1. Sit **beside** _____.

    prepositional phrase: _____

2. I ate an apple **after** _____.

    prepositional phrase: _____

3. He looked **behind** the _____ for his ball.

    prepositional phrase: _____

4. This note is **from** _____.

    prepositional phrase: _____

B. Directions: Find the prepositional phrase in the sentence and cross it
                 out with one horizontal (———) line.

          Example: Mr. Lang sat ~~on a park bench~~.

1. The boy rushed out the door.

2. Place the picture above this oak table.

3. Your skates are in that closet.

4. During the program, several children sang.

5. The family went inside the old church.

Object of the Preposition

The object of the preposition is the **last word** in a prepositional phrase.

    Example: to **school**

        School is the object of the preposition.

    Example: with his little **brother**

        Brother is the object of the preposition.

Label the **O**bject of the **P**reposition by writing **O.P** above it.

                     O.P.
Examples: to school

                     O.P.
           with his brother

A.   Directions: Write an object of the preposition in the blank.

1.   She asked **for** a _____.

2.   The man stood **in** the _____.

3.   Mrs. Bell put the dish **into** the _____.

4.   **Before** a _____, we always buy popcorn.

5.   Kay lives **by** a large _____.

B.   Directions: Find the prepositional phrase in the sentence and cross it
                   out with one horizontal (———) line. Then, write **O.P.**
                   above the object of the preposition.

Remember: **The object of the preposition is the last word in a
                prepositional phrase.**

1.   A bee landed on the flower.

2.   Several dogs barked during the storm.

3.   They often go to the library.

4.   The team ran into the locker room.

5.   Kim fell off her chair.

6.   That horse eats apples from my hand.

FINDING THE SUBJECT AND THE VERB OF A SENTENCE

☞**Subject:** The subject of a sentence is **who** or **what** a sentence is about.

Good news: **A word in a prepositional phrase will not be the subject of a sentence.**

To find the subject, first cross out each prepositional phrase.

Example: The duck swam ~~across the pond~~.

Pond cannot be the subject. *Pond* is in a prepositional phrase, and we have crossed it out. To find the subject, read the remaining words.

The duck swam.

Ask **who** or **what** the sentence is about. The sentence is about a duck. *Duck* is the subject. We place a line under *duck* to show it is the subject.

The <u>duck</u> swam.

Sometimes, there may be several words in front of the subject.
The large white <u>duck</u> swam.

We still are only talking about the duck. We underline only *duck*.

☞**Verb:**

The verb of a sentence is what **happens (or happened)** or what **is (or was)** in a sentence.

Good news: **A word in a prepositional phrase will not be the verb of a sentence.**

To find the verb, first cross out each prepositional phrase. Next, find the subject.   Then, ask what is (was) or is happening (happened) in the sentence.
Example: The <u>duck</u> swam ~~across the pond~~.

What happened in the sentence? What did the duck do? The duck swam. *Swam* is the verb. We underline the verb twice.   The <u>duck</u> <u>swam</u>. 15

Directions: Cross out the prepositional phrase in each sentence. Then, underline the subject once and the verb twice.

Example: Joe played with his friends.

1.   He sits on a stool.

2.   I bumped into a door.

3.   Bob plays in a band.

4.   A ball rolled behind a table.

5.   She swam to the steps.

6.   Butter dripped down his arm.

7.   We walked by the river.

8.   Judy laughed at the playful monkey.

9.   After lunch, the baby naps.

10.   The child slid under the table.

11.   That gift is from her brother.

12.   Peter snacks before dinner.

13.   The children dashed up the steps.

16

Directions: Cross out the prepositional phrase in each sentence. Then, underline the subject once and the verb twice.

Example: Several <u>children</u> <u>skipped</u> ~~to a song~~.

1. Susie lives in a city.

2. They hid behind the sofa.

3. He went into the garage.

4. Sam jumped over a cardboard box.

5. Their dog sleeps under their bed.

6. Mark sat between his parents.

7. A fisherman waded through the water.

8. Her cut was below her right knee.

9. Some fawns walked across a meadow.

10. The package is from Dave's sister.

11. His grandmother often sits beside a window.

12. The three girls shopped with their aunt.

13. A small bee buzzed around the room.

14. We wash our hands before every meal.

Name_____

Date_____

Directions: Cross out **any** prepositional phrase(s) in each sentence. Then, underline the subject once and the verb twice.

Remember: **You may have more than one prepositional phrase in a sentence.**

Example: He went up the escalator with his friend.

1. During the spring, Jane traveled to Texas.

2. Matt lives by a police station on Birch Street.

3. They waded under the bridge for fifteen minutes.

4. Mr. Hunt went into the building and up the elevator.

5. After the race, the girls sat beside their coach.

6. The band marched down the field before a football game.

7. Many bags of groceries lay below the counter.

8. Mrs. Maxwell walked through the door of her office.

9. The letter from Buck fell off the wooden desk.

10. An earthworm crawled across the blade of grass.

11. She placed a star above her name on the paper.

12. Peach yogurt is behind the jam in the refrigerator.

18

Name_____

Date_____

Sometimes a sentence is talking about two or more people or things. This is called a **compound subject**.

       Example: Her dog and ferret play in her room.

1. Cross out any prepositional phrase(s):

       Her dog and ferret play ~~in her room~~.

2. Look for more than one *who* or *what* in the sentence.

       Her <u>dog</u> and <u>ferret</u> play.

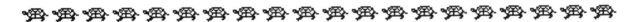

Directions: Cross out **any** prepositional phrase(s) in each sentence. Then, underline the compound subject once and the verb twice.

Remember: **The subject will not be any word in a prepositional phrase.**

       Example: <u>Jacy</u> and his <u>brother</u> <u><u>are</u></u> ~~in a scout troop~~.

1. Spoons and forks are beside the napkins.

2. Paco or Nikki sits behind Ama.

3. Your shoes and socks were under the bed.

4. Either their mother or father reads with them.

5. In March, Lulu and her cousin visited Pandaland.

6. During the race, Dino, Ria, and I finished at the same time.

Sometimes a sentence is talking about two or more people or things. This is called a **compound subject**.

Look for more than one *who* or *what* in the sentence.

🐢 🐢 🐢 🐢 🐢 🐢 🐢 🐢 🐢 🐢 🐢 🐢 🐢 🐢 🐢 🐢 🐢 🐢

Directions: Cross out **any** prepositional phrase(s) in each sentence. Then, underline the compound subject once and the verb twice.

Example: <u>Tara</u> and her <u>dad</u> <u>swim</u> daily.

1. New towels and washcloths are in the bathroom.

2. Miss Cortez and her new boyfriend arrived today.*

3. His brother or sister goes to Colorado during the winter.

4. Her friends and she decorated for the party.

5. Marshmallows and hot dogs are by the fireplace.

6. Several cows and horses rested under some tall trees.

7. Mira and Van walked with Grandma through her flower garden.

8. Mother and I placed pins below the last button of my sweater.

9. Jay, Lali, Kam, and Lana went to the circus.

10. That teacher, the principal, and the secretary meet each Friday.*

*Not all sentences contain prepositional phrases.

Sometimes more than one thing happens (happened) or is (was) in a sentence. This is called a **compound verb**. Two or more verbs make up a compound verb.

Example: The deer looked at us and ran away.

1. Cross out any prepositional phrase(s). Underline the subject once.

The <u>deer</u> looked ~~at us~~ and ran away.

2. Look for more than one thing that happens (happened) or is (was) in the sentence. What did the deer do?

The <u>deer</u> <u>looked</u> ~~at us~~ and <u>ran</u> away.

The deer did two things. First, he *looked* and then he *ran*.

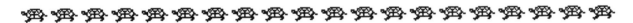

Directions: Cross out **any** prepositional phrase(s) in each sentence. Then, underline the subject once and the compound verb twice.

Remember: **The verb will not be any word in a prepositional phrase.**

Example: <u>They</u> <u>sang</u> and <u>clapped</u> ~~to the music~~.

1. He smiled and waved at us.

2. A glass plate fell and broke into many pieces.

3. A toddler cried and ran to his mother.

4. Jackie laughed and ran across the lawn.

5. A large bug flew to a bush and chewed on a leaf.

Sometimes more than one thing happens (happened) or is (was) in a sentence. This is called a **compound verb**. Two or more verbs make up a compound verb.

Cross out any prepositional phrase(s). Underline the subject once. Look for more than one thing that happens (happened) or is (was) in a sentence.

Example: A fire <u>engine</u> <u>roared</u> ~~around the corner~~ and <u>stopped</u>.

The fire engine did two things. First, it *roared,* and then it *stopped.*

🐢 🐢 🐢 🐢 🐢 🐢 🐢 🐢 🐢 🐢 🐢 🐢 🐢 🐢 🐢 🐢 🐢 🐢

Directions: Cross out **any** prepositional phrase(s) in each sentence. Then, underline the subject once and the compound verb twice.

Remember: **The verb will not be any word in a prepositional phrase.**

Example: Her <u>cat</u> <u>lay</u> ~~on the floor~~ and <u>slept</u>.

1. Tad looked at me and laughed.

2. A baby sucked his hand and grinned.

3. Their uncle went to the store and bought chips.

4. That dog looks mean but is very friendly.

5. They drank cola and ate snacks at the party.

6. Her cousin sings in a choir and plays the fiddle.

7. A monkey sat on a box and scratched himself.

8. Joan stared in the mirror, smiled, and flossed her teeth.

A. **Compound Subject:** Look for more than one *who* or *what* in a sentence.

Directions: Cross out **any** prepositional phrase(s) in each sentence. Then, underline the compound subject once and the verb twice.

Remember: The subject will not be any word in a prepositional phrase.

Example: Her <u>coat</u> and <u>hat</u> <u>are</u> ~~on the floor~~.

1.   Their aunt and uncle live in Denver.

2.   An apple and a banana are on the table.

3.   This doll and suitcase were gifts for her birthday.

4.   After the storm, branches and weeds lay beside the house.

5.   Mom and Dad washed our car during the afternoon.

🐢 🐢 🐢 🐢 🐢 🐢 🐢 🐢 🐢 🐢 🐢 🐢 🐢 🐢 🐢 🐢 🐢 🐢

B. **Compound Verb:** Two or more verbs make up a compound verb.

Directions: Cross out **any** prepositional phrase(s) in each sentence. Then, underline the subject once and the compound verb twice.

Remember: The verb will not be any word in a prepositional phrase.

Example: <u>Miss Kent</u> <u>dug</u> ~~in the ground~~ and <u>planted</u> seeds.

1.   Ira stayed and helped with games.

2.   The model smiled and looked at the crowd.

3.   His friend waters and cuts grass during the summer.

4.   Cal rushed into the post office and bought stamps.

5.   A chicken walked around the barnyard and pecked in the dirt.   23

An imperative sentence gives a **command**.

Example: Sit on this chair.

The person writing or speaking the command usually does not include the word, *you*. However, you realize that the person is telling **you** to do something. We call this *you understood*. *You understood* is written as (You).

To find subject and verb of an imperative sentence, follow these steps:

1. Cross out any prepositional phrase(s).   Sit ~~on this chair~~.

2. Write (You), *you understood*, at the beginning of the sentence.
       (You) Sit ~~on this chair~~.

3. Decide the verb by asking what you are being told to do. Underline the verb twice.
       (You) <u>Sit</u> ~~on this chair~~.

🐢🐢🐢🐢🐢🐢🐢🐢🐢🐢🐢🐢🐢🐢🐢🐢🐢🐢🐢🐢🐢🐢🐢🐢🐢

Directions: Cross out any prepositional phrase(s).   Underline the subject once and the verb twice.

1.   Jump into the water.

2.   Hop on one foot.

3.   Smile for the picture.

4.   Stand in line with me.

5.   Place the soap under the sink.

6.   Please pass this pencil to Mike.

24

Name_____

Date_____

An imperative sentence gives a **command**.

      Example: Sit on this chair.

The person writing or speaking the command usually does not include the word, *you*. However, you realize that the person is telling **you** to do something. We call this *you understood*. *You understood* is written as (You).

To find subject and verb of an imperative sentence, follow these steps:

1.   Cross out any prepositional phrase(s).

      Please give this ~~to your dad~~.

2.   Write (You), *you understood,* at the beginning of the sentence.

      (You)   Please give this ~~to your dad~~.

3.   Decide the verb by asking what you are being told to do. Underline the verb twice.

      (You)   Please <u>give</u> this ~~to your dad~~.

🐢 🐢

Directions: Cross out any prepositional phrase(s). Underline the subject once and the verb twice.

     Remember: Not all sentences contain prepositional phrases.

1. Play with me.

2. Clean your room.

3. Brush your teeth.

4. Wait for us after school.

5. Wash your hands before dinner.

6. Throw the ball to first base.

Name_____   **PREPOSITIONS**
                                              Review
Date_____

Directions: List the twenty-eight prepositions that you have learned.

1. _____   15. _____

2. _____   16. _____

3. _____   17. _____

4. _____   18. _____

5. _____   19. _____

6. _____   20. _____

7. _____   21. _____

8. _____   22. _____

9. _____   23. _____

10. _____   24. _____

11. _____   25. _____

12. _____   26. _____

13. _____   27. _____

14. _____   28. _____

A.   Directions: Write a prepositional phrase.

1. between _____

2. under _____

3. for _____

B.   Directions: Cross out the prepositional phrase. Then, write <u>O. P.</u> above
                   each object of the preposition.

1. She looked through a telescope.

2. After lunch, they went bowling.

3. Several books are lying on the sofa.

C.   Directions: Cross out the prepositional phrase in each sentence.
                   Underline the subject once and the verb twice.

Remember: Ask *who* or *what* the sentence is about to find the subject.
Find what happens (happened) or is (was). This is the verb.
Subject and verb will not be in a prepositional phrase.

Example: Two <u>lizards</u> <u>are</u> ~~in the yard~~.

1. A light hangs above their table.

2. Your mother is in the other room.

3. That frog just jumped into the water.

4. Her brother walked beside us.   27

A. Compound Subject:

Directions: Cross out the prepositional phrase in each sentence. Then, underline the compound subject once and the verb twice.

Remember: **The subject will not be a word in a prepositional phrase.**

1. Barbara and I skipped to the store.

2. His hat and coat were under some newspapers.

3. Toni and her friend sang after dinner.

B. Compound Verb:

Directions: Cross out the prepositional phrase in each sentence. Then, underline the subject once and the compound verb twice.

Remember: **The verb will never be a word in a prepositional phrase.**

1. The kite dipped and soared above the trees.

2. A policeman whistled and pointed at the driver.

3. Before bedtime, I wash my face and brush my teeth.

C. Imperative Sentence:

Directions: Cross out the prepositional phrase in each sentence. Then, underline the subject once and the verb twice.

Remember: **An imperative sentence gives a command.**

1. Stand in this line.

2. Dust under your bed.

3. Put your name on the paper, please.

28

A. Directions: Write a prepositional phrase.

1. across_____

2. up_____

3. below_____

B. Directions: Cross out the prepositional phrase. Then, write <u>O. P.</u> above
each object of the preposition.

1. He ordered tiles from Mexico.

2. This box of candy is old.

3. The groom danced with his new bride.

C. Directions: Cross out the prepositional phrase in each sentence.
Underline the subject once and the verb twice.

Remember: **Ask *who* or *what* the sentence is about to find the subject.**
Find what happens (happened) or is (was). This is the verb.
Subject and verb will not be in a prepositional phrase.

Example: The <u>teenager</u> <u>waved</u> ~~to me~~.

1. Your coat is inside the closet.

2. The ladies walked around the museum.

3. We fished off the pier.

4. At five o'clock, the workers went home.   29

A. Compound Subject:

Directions: Cross out the prepositional phrase in each sentence. Then, underline the compound subject once and the verb twice.

Remember: The subject will not be a word in a prepositional phrase.

1.   A bear and her cub roamed through the woods.

2.   During the rain, Mother and Jack painted.

3.   A doctor and nurse talked beside the water fountain.

B. Compound Verb:

Directions: Cross out the prepositional phrase in each sentence. Then, underline the subject once and the compound verb twice.

Remember: The verb will never be a word in a prepositional phrase.

1.   A first grader ran into the room and shouted.

2.   Their sister washes and curls her hair before school.

3.   He sliced tomatoes and fried them in butter.

C. Imperative Sentence:

Directions: Cross out the prepositional phrase in each sentence. Then, underline the subject once and the verb twice.

Remember: An imperative sentence gives a command.

1. Turn to the left.

2. Hand this mug to that waiter.

3. Please use this carton of eggs.

30

Directions: Cross out any prepositional phrase(s). Underline the subject once and the verb twice.

Example: One ~~of the lambs~~ <u>followed</u> his mother.

1. Jason hid behind a shed.

2. The sky grew dark before the storm.

3. Deep water rushed over the bridge.

4. Several guests lay beside the hotel pool.

5. One of her friends works in a hotel.

6. The water in the pond dropped below five feet.

7. Those girls ride on a bus to the mall.

8. Keep your skates under your bed.

9. That man with three small children is my uncle.

10. During the ice storm, we played cards by the fire.

11. Please come inside the house with me.

12. The runner finished the race and fell on the ground.

13. A package from Fred arrived after lunch.

14. The lady and her son looked for a book at the library.

Name_____ **PREPOSITIONS**
Review

Date_____

Directions: Cross out any prepositional phrase(s). Underline the subject once and the verb twice.

Example: <u>They</u> <u>ride</u> a merry-go-round ~~on Saturdays~~.

1. Sheri caught a fish in Mexico.

2. That garden hose wraps around a metal stand.

3. Bo and Carrie ran through the woods.

4. Before church, they eat at a coffee shop.

5. An enormous white cat slipped out the door.

6. During the game, he hopped on one foot.

7. Dad poured food into our dog's bowl.

8. Several cows went up the large, grassy hill.

9. Mrs. Jackson waved a flag above her head.

10. A ferry comes across the lake every day.

11. The actor took off his wig and smiled.

12. They washed their hands with sudsy soap.

13. Wait for me beside the front door.

14. Each of the contestants walked between two white columns.

**Complete Subject
and
Complete Verb**

Sometimes, you will be asked to find the complete subject and the complete verb of a sentence. This is very easy. Follow these steps.

1. Cross out any prepositional phrases.

2. Underline the subject with one line.

3. Underline the verb with a double line.

4. With a wavy red line, underline everything **before the verb**. This is the complete subject.

5. With a wavy green line, underline the **verb** and everything **after the verb**. This is the complete verb.

   Example: The little girl slid down the slide.

   The little <u>girl</u> **slid** down the slide.
   The verb is *slid*. Separate the sentence here.
   The little <u>girl</u>   **slid** down the slide.
   ~~~~~~~~~~~   ~~~~~~~~~~~~~~~

Complete subject: The little girl   Complete verb: slid down the slide.

🐢 🐢 🐢 🐢 🐢 🐢 🐢 🐢 🐢 🐢 🐢 🐢 🐢 🐢 🐢 🐢 🐢 🐢 🐢

Directions: Cross out any prepositional phrase(s). Underline the subject once and the verb twice. Place a wavy red line under the complete subject and a wavy green line under the complete verb.

   Example: A bowl of cherries is on the table.
   A <u>bowl</u> of cherries <u>is</u> on the table.
   ~~~~~~~~~~~~~~~ ~~~~~~~~~~~~~

1. Two girls played in the park.

2. The boy in the blue sweater is my friend.

3. My little brother cries during his bath.

33

Follow these steps to find the **complete subject** and the **complete verb**.

1. Cross out any prepositional phrases.
2. Underline the subject with one line and the verb with a double line.
3. With a wavy red line, underline everything **before the verb**. This is the complete subject.
4. With a wavy green line, underline the **verb** and everything **after the verb**. This is the complete verb.

> Example: A <u>bug</u> <u>flew</u> ~~into the house~~.
>
> The verb is *flew*. Separate the sentence here.
>
> A <u>bug</u>   <u>**flew**</u> ~~into the house~~.

🐢 🐢 🐢 🐢 🐢 🐢 🐢 🐢 🐢 🐢 🐢 🐢 🐢 🐢 🐢 🐢 🐢 🐢 🐢

Directions: Cross out any prepositional phrase(s). Underline the subject once and the verb twice. Place a red wavy line under the complete subject and a green wavy line under the complete verb.

> Example: Her <u>neighbor</u> <u>is</u> ~~in the army~~.

1. We went to the zoo.

2. Their sister is in college.

3. A large tree grew by the stream.

4. This quarter is for you.

5. A lady at the market gave me an apple.

6. Several brown bunnies sit under our bush.

Date_____

A direct object receives an action.

To find a direct object, do the following steps:

1. Cross out any prepositional phrase(s). Any word in a prepositional phrase will **not** be a direct object.

2. Underline the subject once and the verb twice. Does the verb show an **action**? If the verb shows action, there may be a direct object.

3. Read your subject and verb. Ask yourself if there is an object that would answer *what*.

    Example: Ross <u>made</u> cookies.   Ross made ***what?*** cookies

    The object Ross made is cookies. ***Cookies*** is the direct object.
    Write **D.O.** above a direct object.
    D.O.
    <u>Ross</u> <u>made</u> cookies.

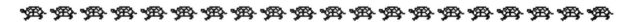

Directions: Cross out any prepositional phrase(s). Underline the subject once and the verb twice. Write <u>D.O.</u> above any direct object.

D.O.
Example: <u>Tim</u> <u>empties</u> his trash ~~on Friday~~.

1. Tyler eats popcorn at the movies.

2. The baby drank juice from a bottle.

3. Lisa splashed water on her face.

4. Her father cut her birthday cake.

35

A direct object receives an action.

To find a direct object, do the following steps:

1. Cross out any prepositional phrase(s).   Any word in a prepositional phrase will **not** be a direct object.

2. Underline the subject once and the verb twice.   Does the verb show an **action**? If the verb shows action, there may be a direct object.

3. Read your subject and verb.   Ask yourself if there is an object that would answer *what*.

D.O.
Example: Joan kicked the football ~~to her brother~~.

Joan kicked what?   *football* Football is the direct object.

🐢 🐢 🐢 🐢 🐢 🐢 🐢 🐢 🐢 🐢 🐢 🐢 🐢 🐢 🐢 🐢 🐢 🐢

Directions: Cross out any prepositional phrase(s). Underline the subject once and the verb twice. Write <u>D.O.</u> above any direct object.

D.O.
Example: They watched television.

1.   She sang a song with her aunt.

2.   The child poured sand into a bucket.

3.   Lance collects baseball cards.

4.   That artist paints pictures of animals.

5.   Mr. Rank bought a gift for his wife.

6.   The plumber fixed a leak in the sink.

CONTRACTIONS

To contract means to become smaller.

Contractions are formed when two or more words are joined together.

you are = you're

When the words are joined, the new word is smaller because a letter or letters have been dropped.

you are = six letters
you're = five letters
a

Where the letter or letters have been dropped, an apostrophe mark (') is placed.

you're

a

Make an apostrophe with a curve in it. Put the apostrophe exactly where the letter or letters have been dropped.

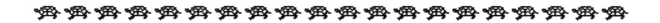

Contractions with **I**:

I am	=	I'm	I will	=	I'll
I have	=	I've			

Contractions with **you**:

you are	=	you're
you will	=	you'll

Contractions with **is**:

he is	=	he's	she is	=	she's
here is	=	here's	what is	=	what's
it is	=	it's	where is	=	where's
that is	=	that's	who is	=	who's
there is	=	there's			

Contractions with **they**:

they are	=	they're
they will	=	they'll

Contractions with **we**:

we are	=	we're
we will	=	we'll

Contractions with **not**:

are not	=	aren't
cannot	=	can't
could not	=	couldn't
did not	=	didn't
does not	=	doesn't
do not	=	don't
had not	=	hadn't
has not	=	hasn't
have not	=	haven't
is not	=	isn't
should not	=	shouldn't
was not	=	wasn't
were not	=	weren't
will not	=	won't
would not	=	wouldn't

38

Name_____   **VERBS**
                                      Contractions
Date_____

Directions: Write the contraction.

1.   I am - _____

2.   I have - _____

3.   I will - _____

4.   it is - _____

5.   he is - _____

6.   she is - _____

7.   who is - _____

8.   what is - _____

9.   where is - _____

10.   here is - _____

11.   there is - _____

12.   they are - _____

13.   they have - _____

VERBS
Contractions

Directions: Write the contraction.

1.   do not - _____

2.   does not - _____

3.   did not - _____

4.   has not - _____

5.   have not - _____

6.   had not - _____

7.   is not - _____

8.   are not - _____

9.   was not - _____

10.   were not - _____

11.   cannot - _____

12.   will not - _____

13.   would not - _____

Name_____ **VERBS**
Contractions

Date_____

Directions: Write the contraction for the words in boldfaced (very black) type.

1. _____ **I will** play with you.

2. _____ Stacey **cannot** come with us.

3. _____ **He is** my dad's boss.

4. _____ Tom **should not** play in the street.

5. _____ **You are** very nice.

6. _____ Janet **does not** like to swing.

7. _____ Mrs. Harmon **is not** here yet.

8. _____ **They are** going to the park today.

9. _____ I **have not** done my chores.

10. _____ **Where is** your brother?

11. _____ **You will** enjoy this game.

12. _____ Paul **did not** leave early.

13. _____ One runner **has not** finished.

Name_____

Date_____

Directions: Write the contraction for the words in boldfaced (very black) type.

1. _____   **They are** having a great time!

2. _____   **It is** raining.

3. _____   The hamster **was not** in its cage.

4. _____   The child **would not** answer.

5. _____   **I am** going to a birthday party.

6. _____   **Do not** go outside without a coat.

7. _____   Tulips **will not** bloom until spring.

8. _____   **They are** going to the park today.

9. _____   That player **did not** score any points.

10. _____   **What is** the highest building in the United Sates?

11. _____   **That is** the funniest story I have ever heard.

12. _____   Those diamonds **are not** real.

42

Name_____   **VERBS**
                                       Contractions
Date_____

A.   Directions: Write the contractions that begin with **you**:

1.   _____   2.   _____

B.   Directions: Write the contractions that begin with **they**:

1.   _____   2.   _____

C.   Directions: Write the contractions that begin with **I**:

1.   _____   2.   _____   3.   _____

D.   Directions: Write the contractions that contain **is**:

1.   _____   4.   _____   7.   _____

2.   _____   5.   _____   8.   _____

3.   _____   6.   _____   9.   _____

E.   Directions: Write the contractions that contain **n't (not)**. To help you,
     the first letter of each contraction is in parentheses ( ).

1.   (a)_____   6.   (d)_____   11.   (s)_____

2.   (c)_____   7.   (h)_____   12.   (w)_____

3.   (c)_____   8.   (h)_____   13.   (w)_____

4.   (d)_____   9.   (h)_____   14.   (w)_____

5.   (d)_____   10. (i)_____   15.   (w)_____

43

It's is a contraction meaning **it is**.   An **apostrophe** is used.

The word **its** is a word used to show that something owns or has something.

>   Example: The car lost **its** wheel.

>   What does the car have? The car has *its* **wheel**.
>   Do **not** use an apostrophe with <u>its</u>.

If you do not remember which word to use, try dividing **it's** into **it is**.

>   Example: The car lost **it is** wheel.

>   That sounds strange!   Now you know to use <u>its</u>.

Directions: Circle the correct word.

1.   Your hair has lost (it's, its) shine.

2.   Today, (it's, its) very cloudy.

3.   (It's, Its) your turn.

4.   The vase fell over on (it's, its) side.

5.   The moose raised (it's, its) head and looked around.

6.   When (it's, its) four o'clock, you may go outside and play.

7.   A large kangaroo raised (it's, its) tail and hopped away.

8.   On Valentine's Day, (it's, its) a custom to give cards.

9.   Take the cake from the oven if (it's, its) baked.

They're/Their/There

They're is a contraction meaning **they are**.   An **apostrophe** is used.

Example: They're finished.

Their is a word used to show that something owns or has something.

Example: The children carried their skis.

What do the children have? The children have *their* **skis.**
Do **not** use an apostrophe with <u>their</u>**.**

There tells **where**.

Example: I want to go *there*.

Sometimes, **there** is used at the beginning of a sentence.

Example: *There* are thirty pennies in this jar.

<u>If you don't remember which word to use, divide **they're** into **they are**.</u>

Example: The children carried **they're** skis.

The children carried **they are** skis.

That doesn't make sense!   Use ***their***.

🐢 **They're** is a contraction meaning **they are.**   An **apostrophe** is used.

Example: *They're* in first grade.

🐢 **Their** is a word used to show that something owns or has something.

Example: *Their* sister is a golfer.

🐢 **There** tells **where.**   Example: I want to go *there.*

Sometimes, **there** is used at the beginning of a sentence.

Example: *There* is a crack in this cup.

🐢🐢🐢🐢🐢🐢🐢🐢🐢🐢🐢🐢🐢🐢🐢🐢🐢🐢🐢🐢🐢🐢🐢

Directions: Circle the correct word in each sentence.

1.   (Their, They're, There) scout leader is Mr. Hines.

2.   Josh's family went (their, they're, there) last summer.

3.   (Their, They're, There) learning about frogs.

4.   After eating lunch, (their, they're, there) father took them to the zoo.

5.   (Their, They're, There) are no ice cubes in the freezer.

6.   During the storm, (their, they're, there) tree blew over.

7.   Did you know (their, they're, there) isn't any ice cream left?

8.   I think that (their, they're, there) leaving on Friday.

9.   They are taking (their, they're, there) cat to a show.

Date_____

🐢 **They're** is a contraction meaning **they are**. An **apostrophe** is used.

🐢 **Their** is a word used to show that something owns or has something.

🐢 **There** tells **where**. Sometimes, **there** is used at the beginning of a sentence.

🐢 🐢

Directions: Circle the correct word in each sentence.

1.   The runners all finished (their, they're, there) race.

2.   (Their, They're, There) will be no school on Monday.

3.   Do you want (their, they're, there) telephone number?

4.   (Their, They're, There) plans have changed.

5.   Those birds chirp when (their, they're, there) nervous.

6.   We went (their, they're, there) last summer.

7.   (Their, They're, There) grandma is coming soon.

8.   (Their, They're, There) the best two-square players.

9.   Some girls left (their, they're, there) papers at home.

10.   I went (their, they're, there) during my spring break.

🐢 **You're** is a contraction for **you are**. An **apostrophe** is used.

    Example: **You're** funny.
         You are funny.

🐢 **Your** is a word used to show that something owns or has something.

    Example: **Your** pencil is on the floor.

        Your will go over to (modify) another word. It will answer <u>what</u>. *Your what?* Your **pencil**!

🐢 If you are not sure which word to use, try reading the sentence using *you are*.

    Examples: You're right!

         You are right!   (This makes sense!)

         You're sister is here.
         You are sister is here. (This doesn't make sense!)
         Your sister is here.   (This is correct!)

🐢🐢🐢🐢🐢🐢🐢🐢🐢🐢🐢🐢🐢🐢🐢🐢🐢🐢🐢🐢🐢🐢

Directions: Circle the correct word in each sentence.

1. Are (you're, your) parents here?

2. (You're, Your) friends are waiting for you.

3. Troy said, "(You're, Your) invited to my party."

4. (You're, Your) lunch is in this bag.

5. (You're, Your) the best artist.

48

🐢 **You're** is a contraction for **you are**.   An **apostrophe** is used.

🐢 **Your** is a word used to show that something owns or has something.

🐢 If you are not sure which word to use, try reading the sentence using *you are*.

    Examples: You're nice!

                 You are nice!   (This makes sense!)

🐢🐢🐢🐢🐢🐢🐢🐢🐢🐢🐢🐢🐢🐢🐢🐢🐢🐢🐢🐢🐢🐢🐢

Directions: Circle the correct word in each sentence.

1.   Does (you're, your) name have an <u>o</u> in it?

2.   Don asked if (you're, your) going with us.

3.   (You're, Your) shoe is under the bed.

4.   (You're, Your) lucky.

5.   Has (you're, your) uncle written a new song?

6.   Are you sure that (you're, your) ready?

7.   (You're, Your) a very good actor, Kelly.

8.   Is (you're, your) last answer 52?

9.   Jackie has (you're, your) bicycle pump.

10.   Next week, (you're, your) allowed to attend the rodeo .

Name_____

Date_____

A. Directions: Write **it's** or **its** in the blank.

1. Jordan said, "_____ time to eat."

2. The book had been damaged; _____ pages were torn.

3. _____ cold outside!

4. The worm curled _____ tail around a piece of grass.

B. Directions: Write **they're**, **their**, or **there** in the blank.

1. Has _____ dog been found?

2. _____ waiting for a phone call.

3. _____ is no cereal for breakfast.

4. _____ last house had a fireplace.

5. Gail doesn't know if _____ coming to the party.

C. Directions: Write **you're** or **your** in the blank.

1. _____ standing on my foot!

2. _____ kite is crashing!

3. Yesterday, _____ poem won a contest.

4. I think that _____ a good friend.

50

🐢**Can** means **to be able to**.

      Example: **Can** you fix my bike?

🐢**May** sometimes **asks permission**.

      Example: **May** I go with you?

May sometimes **gives permission.**

      Example: You **may** eat outside today.

May sometimes suggests a possibility.

      Example: Betty **may** go to the beach soon.

🐢🐢🐢🐢🐢🐢🐢🐢🐢🐢🐢🐢🐢🐢🐢🐢🐢🐢🐢🐢🐢🐢🐢🐢🐢

Directions: Write **can** or **may** in the blank.

1. _____ you hold this for me?

2. You _____ begin now.

3. _____ Sarah and I make a card?

4. You _____ have to wait for a bus.

5. _____ this watch be repaired?

6. _____ I say something?

VERBS

The verb in a sentence shows an action or says a fact.

A. ACTION VERBS:

        Examples: Micah **plays** a guitar.
                      Devi **laughs** often.
                      A mouse **darted** across the floor.
                      Dad **helped** me with the project.

B. STATE OF BEING VERBS:

1. The verb, ***to be***, simply states a fact. It is called a state of being verb.
2. The forms of *to be* are: <u>**is**</u>, <u>**am**</u>, <u>**are**</u>, <u>**was**</u>, <u>**were**</u>, <u>**be**</u>, <u>**being**</u>, <u>**been**</u>.

    a. For telling present time:

        Use **am** with the pronoun, <u>I</u>.
            Example: I **am** a good singer.

        Use **is** when the subject is only one.
            Example: He **is** a great rider.

        Use **are** when the subject is <u>you</u>.
            Example: You **are** a nice friend.

        Use **are** when the subject is more than one.
            Examples: The bananas **are** ripe.
                      Aren and Tito **are** in the kitchen.

    b. For telling past time:

        Use **was** for only one.
            Examples: I **was** scared.
                    A chair **was** on the patio.

        Use **were** when the subject is more than one.
            Examples: Her keys **were** lost.
                    Kami and her sister **were** tired.

Date_____

Some verbs show action.

Directions: Write an action verb on the line; then, draw a picture to show
your sentence.

1.   Dad _____ the floor.

2.   His sister _____ her car.

3.   A man _____ the trees.

4.   He _____ in the afternoon.

Name_____

Date_____

VERBS
Action

Directions: In the blank, write <u>Yes</u> if the boldfaced word shows action.
Write <u>No</u> if the boldfaced verb does not show action.

Example: ____<u>No</u>____ Her hair **is** curly.

1. _____ A golfer **swung** the club.

2. _____ He **climbs** trees by a small pond.

3. _____ Their tricycles **are** in the driveway.

4. _____ Mother **plants** flowers in her garden.

5. _____ Several frogs **leaped** into the water.

6. _____ All of the workers **were** very hungry.

7. _____ Janet **draws** cartoons.

8. _____ Brian **was** the last one on the stage.

9. _____ A hummingbird **flaps** his wings fast.

10. _____ The children **clapped** their hands excitedly.

11. _____ Joe's brothers and sisters **chop** wood in the winter.

12. _____ A special doll **is** on her bed.

54

Name_____ **VERBS**
Action

Date_____

Directions: In the blank, write <u>Yes</u> if the boldfaced word shows action.
Write <u>No</u> if the boldfaced verb does not show action.

Example: _____Yes_____ A cow **chews** its cud.

1. _____ A student **raised** his hand.

2. _____ Her uncle **is** a policeman.

3. _____ Mrs. Kent always **smiles** at us.

4. _____ Some flour **spilled** on the counter.

5. _____ I **am** in the fourth grade.

6. _____ That jet **lands** at the airport every Friday.

7. _____ A bowler **rolled** his ball too hard.

8. _____ Two bags of candy **were** on the table.

9. _____ Several girls **jump** rope each afternoon.

10. _____ Tyler **asked** a question.

11. _____ Joan's father **was** sick last week.

12. _____ A squirrel **gathers** acorns.

Past tense means time that has happened.

      Examples: Susie **walked** to the store.   (It already happened.)

              We **ran** in a race.   (It already happened.)

🐢 A regular verb adds **ed** to the verb to form the past tense.

      Examples: to hop   =   hop**ped**
                  to stay   =   stay**ed**
                  to cry   =   cri**ed**

🐢 An irregular verb does not add **ed** to form the past tense.

      Examples: to swim   =   swam
                  to fly   =   flew
                  to bring   =   brought

🐢🐢🐢🐢🐢🐢🐢🐢🐢🐢🐢🐢🐢🐢🐢🐢🐢🐢🐢🐢🐢🐢🐢

Directions: Write the past tense of each verb.

1. (to talk)   Steven _____ to his brother about the problem.

2. (to smile)   The baby _____ at us.

3. (to sing)   We _____ a new song.

4. (to jump)   Five children _____ into the wading pool at the same time.

5. (to cook)   We _____ hot dogs on the grill.

6. (to find)   Yesterday, I _____ a dime in my pocket.

7. (to laugh)   The crowd _____ at the seal act.

Past tense means time that has happened.

Example: He **sent** a letter.

🐢 A regular verb adds **ed** to the verb to form the past tense.

Examples: to stop = stop**ped**

to whine = whin**ed**

🐢 An irregular verb does not add **ed** to form the past tense.

Examples: to leave = left

to see = saw

🐢🐢🐢🐢🐢🐢🐢🐢🐢🐢🐢🐢🐢🐢🐢🐢🐢🐢🐢🐢🐢🐢🐢🐢

Directions: Write the past tense of each verb. Circle any regular verb.

Remember: You will add ed to form the past tense of regular verbs.

1. to dance - _____

2. to call - _____

3. to go - _____

4. to lock - _____

5. to fall - _____

6. to walk - _____

7. to yell - _____

8. to clean - _____

9. to drink - _____

10. to live - _____

11. to make - _____

12. to like - _____

13. to eat - _____

14. to wash - _____

15. to ride - _____

16. to rub - _____

HELPING VERBS

These verbs help another verb. They are called helping verbs.

do	has	may	can	could	is	was	be
does	have	might	shall	should	am	were	being
did	had	must	will	would	are		been

🐢Sometimes, a verb on this list can stand **alone** in a sentence. This is called the **main verb**.

Example: Sally is my cousin.   (main verb)

🐢Sometimes, **one or more** verbs on this list will be **in front of** another verb. This is called a **verb phrase**.

Example: Sharon is **visiting** her grandpa.   (helping verb)

VERB PHRASE	=	HELPING VERB(S)	+	MAIN VERB
can go	=	can	+	go
had worked	=	had	+	worked
was broken	=	was	+	broken
should have stayed	=	should have	+	stayed

🐢The helping verb or verbs may be beside the main verb.

Example: Her sister **has shopped** all day.

🐢The helping verb or verbs may not be beside the main verb.

Example: Her sister **has** already **shopped** for three hours.

The helping verb or verbs may not be beside the main verb if the sentence asks a question.

58   Example: **Has** her sister **shopped** all day?

Name_____

Date_____

Directions: Write <u>H.V.</u> if the boldfaced verb is a helping verb in the
sentence. Write <u>M.V.</u> if the boldfaced verb is the main verb.

  Example: A. <u> M.V. </u>   **Do** it yourself.

    B. <u> H.V. </u>   **Do** you <u>want</u> to play?

1. A. _____   Keith **does** his chores each day.

  B. _____   Mrs. Frame **does** <u>like</u> to sleep late.

2. A. _____   Jeff **has** a cold.

  B. _____   She **has** <u>driven</u> her dad's car to work.

3. A. _____   Two boys **were** <u>riding</u> bikes.

  B. _____   Their sundaes **were** good.

4. A. _____   Yes, I **can**!

  B. _____   She **can** <u>twirl</u> a baton.

5. A. _____   A plumber **is** <u>fixing</u> our sink.

  B. _____   She **is** the youngest child in the family.

6. A. _____   **Am** I <u>invited</u> to your party?

  B. _____   I **am** nine years old.   59

Name_____   **VERBS**
                                        Helping Verbs
Date_____

Directions: Unscramble the twenty-three helping verbs.

1.   codul - _____   14.   ma - _____

2.   si - _____   15.   acn - _____

3.   ear - _____   16.   lsahl - _____

4.   sode - _____   17.   eb - _____

5.   sah - _____   18.   idd - _____

6.   stum - _____   19.   dulow - _____

7.   nebe - _____   20.   adh - _____

8.   wsa - _____   21.   od - _____

9.   sdohul - _____   22.   vahe - _____

10. reew - _____   23.   gneib - _____

11. liwl - _____

12. yam - _____

13. gitmh - _____

60

Name_____   **VERBS**
                                         Helping Verbs
Date_____

A. Directions: Write the three helping verbs that begin with <u>d</u>:

1. _____   2. _____   3. _____

B. Directions: Write the three helping verbs that begin with <u>h</u>:

1. _____   2. _____   3. _____

C. Directions: Write the three helping verbs that begin with <u>m</u>:

1. _____   2. _____   3. _____

D. Directions: Write the three helping verbs that end with <u>ould</u>:

1. _____   2. _____   3. _____

E. Directions: Write the forms of the verb, <u>to be</u>:

1. _____   2. _____   3. _____

4. _____   5. _____   6. _____

7. _____   8. _____

F. Directions: Write the other three helping verbs on the list:

1. _____   2. _____   3. _____

Name_____

Date_____

Directions: The main verb has been underlined with a double line.
Underline the helping verb with a double line.   Then, write
the verb phrase on the line.

Example: Your brush **is lying** on the bed.   ____is lying____

1.   A bug has <u>crawled</u> up the wall.   _____

2.   Mother may <u>buy</u> a suit.   _____

3.   One of the boys had <u>seen</u> a snake.   _____

4.   I shall <u>bake</u> bread today.   _____

5.   Their neighbors are <u>camping</u>.   _____

6.   We should <u>help</u> you.   _____

7.   Dan was <u>picking</u> tomatoes.   _____

8.   They must <u>clean</u> their bedrooms.   _____

9.   Grandma might <u>like</u> this book.   _____

10.   She can <u>eat</u> three pieces of pizza.   _____

11.   His sisters have <u>made</u> breakfast.   _____

12.   We will <u>leave</u> in a minute.   _____

13.   Do you <u>give</u> Valentine cards?   _____

62

Not isn't a verb. **Not** is an adverb. **Not** is never part of a verb phrase.

In a contraction, box **n't**.   Example: doesn't

To keep from underlining **not** as part of a verb phrase, *box it.*
     Example: The wind wasnotblowing.

🐢 🐢

Directions: The main verb has been underlined with a double line.
                    Underline the helping verb with a double line.   Then, write
                    the verb phrase on the line.

     Example: Mark **has** not paid his bill.   ____has paid____

Remember: Be sure to box *not*.

1.   I did not finish the test.   _____

2.   Bob isn't working today.   _____

3.   The child would not sit still.   _____

4.   You may not stand on the bus.   _____

5.   It hasn't snowed this winter.   _____

6.   The children hadn't played long.   _____

7.   We aren't going until Monday.   _____

8.   Fran cannot find her shoe.   _____

9.   Shouldn't we wait for you?   _____

A verb phrase may contain **more than one** helping verb.

Example: Jeremy **may be** batting next.

🐢 🐢

Directions: Underline the subject once and the verb phrase twice.

1.   The driver should have stopped sooner.

2.   Their roof was being repaired.

3.   Her father may have left.

4.   Our dog must have chewed your slippers.

🐢 🐢

**Review: To find the subject of the sentence, ask about who or
what the sentence is talking.
To help find subject and verb, cross out any
prepositional phrase(s).**

Example: ~~During the storm~~, a chair had fallen ~~into the pool~~.

1.   Two raccoons were drinking from a stream.

2.   They had blown bubbles with special wands.

3.   Mom has been given a present for her birthday.

4.   After the blizzard, snow was scraped from the roads.

5.   The team may be going to Denver for a final game.

6.   The toddler would not share his toys with his friends.

64

IRREGULAR VERBS

Infinitive	Present	Past	Present Participle	Past Participle*
To be	is, am, are	**was, were**	being	**been**
To begin	begin(s)	**began**	beginning	**begun**
To break	break(s)	**broke**	breaking	**broken**
To bring	bring(s)	**brought**	bringing	**brought**
To buy	buy(s)	**bought**	buying	**bought**
To choose	choose(s)	**chose**	choosing	**chosen**
To come	come(s)	**came**	coming	**come**
To dig	dig(s)	**dug**	digging	**dug**
To do	do, does	**did**	doing	**done**
To drink	drink(s)	**drank**	drinking	**drunk**
To drive	drive(s)	**drove**	driving	**driven**
To eat	eat(s)	**ate**	eating	**eaten**
To fall	fall(s)	**fell**	falling	**fallen**
To find	find(s)	**found**	finding	**found**
To fly	fly, flies	**flew**	flying	**flown**
To freeze	freeze(s)	**froze**	freezing	**frozen**
To get	get(s)	**got**	getting	**gotten**
To give	give(s)	**gave**	giving	**given**
To go	go, goes	**went**	going	**gone**
To grow	grow(s)	**grew**	growing	**grown**
To know	know(s)	**knew**	knowing	**known**
To leave	leave(s)	**left**	leaving	**left**

65

Infinitive	Present	Past	Present Participle	Past Participle*
To ride	ride(s)	**rode**	riding	**ridden**
To ring	ring(s)	**rang**	ringing	**rung**
To rise	rise(s)	**rose**	rising	**risen**
To run	run(s)	**ran**	running	**run**
To see	see(s)	**saw**	seeing	**seen**
To send	send(s)	**sent**	sending	**sent**
To set	set(s)	**set**	setting	**set**
To shake	shake(s)	**shook**	shaking	**shaken**
To sing	sing(s)	**sang**	singing	**sung**
To sink	sink(s)	**sank**	sinking	**sunk**
To sit	sit(s)	**sat**	sitting	**sat**
To speak	speak(s)	**spoke**	speaking	**spoken**
To stand	stand(s)	**stood**	standing	**stood**
To steal	steal(s)	**stole**	stealing	**stolen**
To swim	swim(s)	**swam**	swimming	**swum**
To swing	swing(s)	**swung**	swinging	**swung**
To swear	swear(s)	**swore**	swearing	**sworn**
To take	take(s)	**took**	taking	**taken**
To teach	teach(es)	**taught**	teaching	**taught**
To throw	throw(s)	**threw**	throwing	**thrown**
To wear	wear(s)	**wore**	wearing	**worn**
To write	write(s)	**wrote**	writing	**written**

---

*Uses a helping verb such as <u>has</u>, <u>have</u>, <u>had</u>. Other helping verbs such as *was* or *were* may also be used.

66

Name_____

Date_____

Directions: Write the past participle form of the following verb infinitives:
(Use *has*, *have*, or *had* with the word.)

Example: to set -   __had set__

1. to do - _____

2. to leave - _____

3. to teach - _____

4. to know - _____

5. to drink - _____

6. to bring - _____

7. to swear - _____

8. to choose - _____

9. to throw - _____

10. to steal - _____

11. to shake - _____

12. to write - _____

13. to fall - _____

14. to sit - _____

15. to eat - _____

16. to see - _____

17. to go - _____

18. to sing - _____

19. to ride - _____

20. to swim - _____

21. to grow - _____

22. to dig - _____

23. to fly - _____

24. to rise - _____

Name_____   **VERBS**
                                              Irregular Verbs
Date_____

Directions: Write the past participle form of the following verb infinitives:
              (Use *has*, *have*, or *had* with the word.)

              Example: to ride -   __had ridden__

1. to stand - _____   13. to run - _____

2. to begin - _____   14. to set - _____

3. to swing - _____   15. to dig - _____

4. to freeze - _____   16. to take - _____

5. to drive - _____   17. to be - _____

6. to break - _____   18. to find - _____

7. to sink - _____   19. to wear - _____

8. to come - _____   20. to buy - _____

9. to give - _____   21. to get - _____

10. to swim - _____   22. to write - _____

11. to speak - _____   23. to see - _____

12. to send - _____   24. to ring - _____

Name_____

Date_____

Directions: Underline the correct verb with double lines.

    Example: A <u>boy</u> **<u>had</u>** (brang, <u>brought</u>) a snake.

1.   <u>Ellen</u> **<u>has</u>** (broke, broken) her finger.

2.   <u>I</u> **<u>have</u>** (bought, boughten) a ruler.

3.   <u>Ice</u> **<u>had</u>** (froze, frozen) on the pond.

4.   <u>We</u> **<u>have</u>** (written, wrote) letters.

5.   During breakfast, <u>he</u> **<u>had</u>** (ate, eaten) all of the cereal.

6.   <u>Jake</u> **<u>has</u>** (given, gave) his basketball to a friend.

7.   Several <u>kittens</u> **<u>have</u>** (drank, drunk) milk.

8.   <u>Snow</u> **<u>had</u>** (fell, fallen) during the night.

9.   <u>Jan</u> and <u>David</u> **<u>have</u>** (flown, flew) to Idaho.

10.   <u>One</u> of the dogs **<u>has</u>** (run, ran) into the street.

11.   His <u>sister</u> **<u>had</u>** (spoke, spoken) to him harshly.

12.   Bob's <u>brothers</u> **<u>have</u>** (taken, took) a taxi.

13.   Our <u>bus</u> **<u>had</u>** (came, come) early.

Directions: Underline the correct verb with double lines.

Example: He **has** (sang, **sung**) a solo.

1. Marcie **had** (swang, swung) for an hour.

2. I **have** never (ridden, rode) on a subway.

3. The pitcher **should have** (thrown, threw) the ball to first base.

4. Her watch **may have been** (stole, stolen).

5. Five robins **have** (flew, flown) to that branch.

6. He **has** (rang, rung) the buzzer three times.

7. Sally **had** (gave, given) the cashier three dimes.

8. They **must have** (went, gone) somewhere.

9. Both Joan and Brian **had** (run, ran) a mile.

10. One bear **must have** (ate, eaten) too much honey.

11. **Have** you (seen, saw) that video about snakes?

12. The injured person **had been** (took, taken) to the hospital.

13. Mr. Kent **should have** (bought, boughten) another car.

Name_____   **VERBS**
                                                          Irregular Verbs

Date_____

Directions: Underline the subject once and the verb phrase twice.

      Example: <u>They</u> <u>had</u> (rode, <u>ridden</u>) two miles.

1.   Their choir had (sang, sung) two songs.

2.   The taxi has (came, come).

3.   He had (stolen, stole) third base.

4.   A witness has (swore, sworn) an oath.

5.   The ladies have (spoke, spoken).

6.   Ken has (ate, eaten) two hot dogs.

7.   Her sister had (drank, drunk) several milkshakes.

8.   Many birds have (flew, flown) by here.

9.   These steaks were (froze, frozen) last week.

10.   Mindy had (fell, fallen) down.

11.   The coach must have (went, gone) early.

12.   I should have (knew, known) the answer.

13.   Some gloves had been (left, leaved) behind.   71

VERB TENSES

➡ **Present Tense:**

Tense means time. **Present tense means present time.** Although present can mean now, it is easier to use "today" to help you remember. Present tense **never** has a helping verb. To form the present tense, remove *to* from the infinitive:

1. **If the subject is singular (one), add <u>s</u> to the verb.** (**<u>es</u>** to some)

   to wave:　　The <u>baby waves</u> to everybody.　(one child)
   　　　　　　He <u>does</u> exercises.　　　　　　(one boy)

2. **If the subject is <u>you</u>, remove the *to* from the infinitive.**

   to need:　**You need** a bath.

3. **If the subject is <u>I</u>, remove the *to* from the infinitive.**

   to need:　**I need** a bath.

4. **If the subject is <u>PLURAL</u> (more than one), remove the *to* from the infinitive.**

   to need:　Those **children need** baths.

➡ **Past Tense:**

Past tense indicates that which has happened. Although past can mean a second ago, it is easier to use the term, "yesterday." Past tense **never** has a helping verb.

1. **To form the past tense of a regular verb, add <u>ed</u> to the verb.**
   to fix:　fix**ed**　　　　Mom <u>fix**ed**</u> the stereo.

2. **To form the past tense of an irregular verb, change the verb to its correct form.**
   to bring:　**brought**　　<u>Kent **brought**</u> his dog along.

➡ **Future Tense:**

Future tense indicates time yet to happen. There are two helping verbs that indicate future tense: *shall* and *will*. Future may be any time yet to occur. To make it easier, we shall use "tomorrow" as a guide.
   to go:　　<u>I</u> **shall go** to a movie.

　　　　　　His <u>sister</u> **will go** to the mall tomorrow

A.   Directions: Write a complete sentence to answer each question.

1.   Write a sentence telling something you did yesterday.

   Yesterday,_____

   This is the **past tense**.

2.   Write a complete sentence telling something you will do tonight.

   Tonight,_____

   This is the **future tense**.

3.   Write a complete sentence telling something that you do every day.

   Every day,_____

   This is the **present tense**.

B.   Directions: Write a complete sentence to answer each question.

1.   What will a friend and you do next week?   **(future tense)**

   _____

2.   What did a friend and you do last week?   **(past tense)**

   _____

Name_____   **VERBS**
                                                Tenses
Date_____

Directions: Read each sentence.   The verb or verb phrase has been
                 underlined for you. Write the tense of the verb on each line.

Remember: The verb tenses are *present*, *past*, and *future*.

Example: _____past_____   A clown <u>juggled</u> three balls.

1. _____   Their car <u>broke</u> down.

2. _____   Sarah <u>rides</u> her bike every day.

3. _____   They <u>will go</u> grocery shopping.

4. _____   She <u>frosted</u> a cake for her friend.

5. _____   I <u>shall try</u> to help you.

6. _____   Mary's cousin <u>races</u> cars.

7. _____   Jack <u>sewed</u> a button on his jacket.

8. _____   They <u>paint</u> mailboxes for extra
                                 money.

9. _____   The bus <u>will arrive</u> soon.

10. _____   The umpire <u>yelled</u>, "Strike!"

11. _____   Jody and I <u>buy</u> lunch at a deli.

74

Name_____

Date_____

Directions: Read each sentence. The subject and verb/verb phrase have been underlined for you. Write the tense of the verb on each line.

Remember: The verb tenses are *present*, *past*, and *future*.

Example: _____future_____ I shall give you some candy.

1. _____ Lanzo loves his dog.

2. _____ Lanzo loved going to Happyland.

3. _____ Lanzo will love his new house.

1. _____ His sisters skate on the sidewalk.

2. _____ His sisters skated yesterday.

3. _____ His sisters will skate with me tomorrow.

1. _____ Loni will bake cookies tonight.

2. _____ Loni baked a cake yesterday.

3. _____ Loni bakes nearly every week.

Directions: Cross out any prepositional phrases. Underline the subject once and the verb/verb phrase twice. On the line provided, write the tense: *present*, *past*, or *future*.

to look:

1. _____   They looked at the sunset.

2. _____   He looks sad.

3. _____   Dad will look for another car.

to sit:

1. _____   Grandpa sits on the porch.

2. _____   Tom will sit beside me.

3. _____   Baseball players sat by the dugout.

to speak:

1. _____   Mrs. Martin will speak at a meeting.

2. _____   He spoke to me.

3. _____   Scott speaks slowly.

to sing:

1. _____   They sing in the car.

2. _____   She will sing by herself.

3. _____   The group sang for ten minutes.

SUBJECT-VERB AGREEMENT

Rules:
A. If the subject is singular (one), add s to the verb.

>   Example: A <u>fish</u> <u>swim**s**</u>.

We will continue to **cross out prepositional phrases** to help find the subject. Then, it will be easier to make the verb agree.

>   One of the girls (race, races) every day.

The prepositional phrase is ~~of the girls~~. Therefore, ***girls*** cannot be the subject.

>   <u>One</u> ~~of the girls~~ (race, <u>races</u>) every day.   (***One*** is the subject!)

1. Some ***irregular*** verbs completely change form for the present tense.
    Examples: to have: My <u>friend</u> **has** a hamster.
                   to be: Her <u>brother</u> **is** funny.

2. Do **not** add s to a verb after *I.*
    Example: <u>I</u> <u>want</u> a sandwich.

3. Do **not** add s to a verb after ***you.***
    Example: <u>You</u> <u>drink</u> your milk fast.

B. If the subject is plural (more than one), do NOT add s to the verb.

>   Examples: Some <u>babies</u> <u>nap</u> every afternoon.
>
>   Several <u>children</u> <u>eat</u> their snacks outside.

Sometimes, the subject is compound; do not add s if the subjects are joined by ***and.***

>   Example: My <u>friend</u> and <u>I</u> <u>walk</u> home together.

However: Some irregular verbs completely change form for the present tense.

>   Example: <u>Sundaes</u> <u>are</u> good.

Name_____

Date_____

If the subject is singular (one), add s to the verb.

Example: A <u>snake</u> <u>lives</u> in a hole.

A. Directions: Write a sentence that tells what each animal does.

1.   A cat _____.

2.   A bear _____.

3.   A cow _____.

4.   A turtle _____.

5.   A dog _____.

B. Directions: Complete each sentence.
   After I, do not add s to the verb in the present tense.

1.   Often, I_____.

2.   Every summer, I_____.

C. Directions: Complete each sentence.
   After you, do not add s to the verb in the present tense.

1.   Every day, you_____.

2.   Every week, you_____.

78

A. If the subject is singular (one), add s to the verb.

  Do **not** add s to a verb after *I* or *you.*
  Some verbs like *to have* and *to be* totally change forms.

B. If the subject is plural (more than one), do NOT add s to the verb.

  Some irregular verbs like *to be* completely change form.

Directions: Cross out any prepositional phrases. Underline the subject once and the verb twice.

1. Mom (tape, tapes) some programs.

2. Our dogs (dig, digs) in the yard.

3. She always (lie, lies) on her tummy.

4. I (swing, swings) during recess.

5. Katie (tell, tells) funny stories.

6. Mike (do, does) his chores carefully.

7. Those children (play, plays) after lunch.

8. Bob and Tammy (wash, washes) their van.

9. One of the boys (walk, walks) home with his brother.

A.   If the subject is singular (one), add s to the verb.

Do **not** add s to a verb after *I* or *you.*
Some verbs like *to have* and *to be* totally change forms.

B.   If the subject is plural (more than one), do NOT add s to the verb.

Some irregular verbs like *to be* completely change form.

Directions: Cross out any prepositional phrases. Underline the subject once and the verb twice.

1.   I (like, likes) juice.

2.   Dad (buy, buys) ice cream cones for us.

3.   You (clean, cleans) your room well.

4.   Skunks (smell, smells) bad.

5.   A tent (cover, covers) their picnic area.

6.   She (write, writes) her name in cursive.

7.   Fred and Bonnie (shop, shops) every week.

8.   One of the teddy bears (is, are) mine.

Name_____   **VERBS**
                                          Review

Date_____

A. Contractions:

Directions: Write the contraction in the space provided.

1. I have - _____   5. is not - _____

2. I am - _____   6. have not - _____

3. cannot - _____   7. she is - _____

4. they are - _____   8. will not - _____

B.   It's/Its   They're/There/Their   You're/Your:

Directions: Circle the correct word.

1. (You're, Your) not supposed to leave.

2. Has (they're, there, their) cat come home?

3. (It's, Its) time to eat.

4. (They're, There, Their) toasting marshmallows.

5. (You're, Your) bike has been moved.

6. (They're, There, Their) are ten dimes in a dollar.

7. Did you know that (they're, there, their) in a play?

8. A gerbil was running around in (it's, its) cage.

C. Can/May:

Directions: Circle the correct word.

1.   (Can, May) I play with you?

2.   Bob (can, may) jump nearly six feet.

3.   (Can, May) John and I go there?

4.   I (can, may) finish this later.

D.   State of Being:

Directions: Use *is*, *am*, *are*, *was*, or *were* to fill in the blanks.

Present: 1.   I _____ nice.

2.   Honey _____ sweet.

3.   We _____ good students.

Past: 1.   Pat _____ the winner.

2.   The judges _____ from Kansas.

E. Helping (Auxiliary) Verbs:

Directions: List the twenty-three helping verbs.

1. d _   7. m _ _   13. c _ _   19. w _ _

2. d _ _ _   8. m _ _ _ _   14. s _ _ _ _   20. w _ _ _

3. d _ _   9. m _ _ _   15. w _ _ _   21. b _

4. h _ _   10. c _ _ _ _   16. i _   22. b _ _ _ _ _

5. h _ _ _   11. s _ _ _ _ _   17. a _   23. b _ _ _

6. h _ _   12. w _ _ _ _   18. a _ _

F. Helping or Main Verb?:

Directions: Write the helping verb(s) on the first line; write the main verb on the second line.

1. <u>Ben</u> is running a race.   _____   _____

2. One <u>boy</u> had eaten
   three hot dogs.   _____   _____

3. A <u>note</u> was written
   quickly.   _____   _____

4. The <u>rain</u> must have
   stopped.   _____   _____

Name_____   **VERBS**
                                                  Review

Date_____

G. Action?:

Directions: Write <u>Yes</u> if the boldfaced verb shows action; write <u>No</u> if the boldfaced verb does not show action.

1. _____   The elephant **lifted** his trunk.

2. _____   Several bees **buzzed** around her head.

3. _____   I **am** a good swimmer.

4. _____   Mike **gave** his friend some cookies.

5. _____   Sheena **is** in fifth grade.

H.   Regular or Irregular:

Directions: Write the past and past participle in the blank. Then, answer the question.

1. (to brush) Yesterday, I _____ my dog.

    I had _____ my teeth before bedtime.

    To brush is a regular verb if you added *ed.* Is *to brush* a regular or an irregular verb? _____

2. (to throw) Yesterday, she _____ away her sneakers.

    Trina has _____ the ball to her little sister.

    To throw is a regular verb if you added *ed.* Is *to throw* a regular or an irregular verb? _____

84

Name_____ **VERBS**
Review

Date_____

I. Subject/Verb:

Directions: Cross out any prepositional phrase(s). Underline the
subject once and the verb/verb phrase twice.

1. They live by a farm.

2. Larry bit his tongue.

3. Her dad drives a bus in the city.

4. Some girls are sitting under a tree.

5. Betty stayed with her aunt for a week.

6. Will you help me?

J. Irregular Verbs:

Directions: Cross out any prepositional phrase(s). Underline the
subject once and the verb or verb phrase twice.

1. Their mom has (flew, flown) to Texas.

2. Mary had (brung, brought) a sack lunch.

3. You should have (come, came) earlier.

4. Mrs. Cann was (chose, chosen) the winner.

5. I have (drunk, drank) too much ginger ale.

6. They have (eaten, ate) pancakes for breakfast.

K. Tenses:

Directions: Write the tense of the boldfaced verb.

Remember: The tenses are *present*, *past*, and *future*.

1. _____   Kay **likes** ice cream.

2. _____   He **hopped** on one foot.

3. _____   I **shall sit** here.

4. _____   Jo's brothers **go** to bed at 8:00.

5. _____   The clerk **will give** you change.

6. _____   The bell **rang**.

L.   Subject/Verb Agreement:

Directions: Circle the correct verb.

1.   The baby (sleep, sleeps) in a crib.

2.   Those cooks (give, gives) lessons.

3.   He (lifts, lift) weights.

4.   Our dog (play, plays) with our cat.

5.   Many singers (perform, performs) at the fair.

6.   Debra and Lori (is, are) friends.

Name_____

Date_____

A **noun** names a person, a place, or a thing.

🐢 🐢 🐢 🐢 🐢 🐢 🐢 🐢 🐢 🐢 🐢 🐢 🐢 🐢 🐢 🐢 🐢 🐢

Directions: Read each sentence and draw a picture.

1. A person is a **noun**. Draw a picture of someone in your family.

2. A place is a **noun**. Draw a picture of where you live.

3. A thing is a **noun**. Draw a picture of something that you really like.

Name_____

Date_____

A **noun** names a person, a place, or a thing.

🐢 🐢 🐢 🐢 🐢 🐢 🐢 🐢 🐢 🐢 🐢 🐢 🐢 🐢 🐢 🐢 🐢 🐢

Directions: Write a noun that fits in the meaning of each sentence.

1.   An object in this room is a (an) _____.
                                                         (noun)

2.   A part of my head is my _____.
                                              (noun)

3.   In the summer, I like to go to a (an) _____.
                                                              (noun)

4.   My _____ is very funny.
                  (noun)

5.   My family lives in a (an) _____.
                                            (noun)

6.   I really like my _____.
                               (noun)

7.   Something I hold in my hand is a (an) _____.
                                                              (noun)

8.   I might see a (an) _____ at the zoo.
                                (noun)

88

Name_____

Date_____

A **noun** names a person, a place, or a thing.

🐢 🐢 🐢 🐢 🐢 🐢 🐢 🐢 🐢 🐢 🐢 🐢 🐢 🐢 🐢 🐢 🐢 🐢

Directions: Write the answers.

1.   Objects are nouns.   Name two objects that are round.

_____   _____

2.   People are nouns. Name three people you know.

_____   _____   _____

3.   Places are nouns.   Name two places you like to go.

_____   _____

4.   Things that you can see are nouns. Name ten things you can see now.

_____   _____

_____   _____

_____   _____

_____   _____

_____   _____

89

A **common noun** does not name a specific person, place, or thing.

Most nouns are common.   *Example:* football   thumb

Do not capitalize a common noun.

If a type of noun is given, it is still common.   *Example:* dog   collie

A **proper noun** names a **specific** person, place, or thing. **Capitalize** a proper noun.

Example: lake   **Linx Lake**

🐢🐢🐢🐢🐢🐢🐢🐢🐢🐢🐢🐢🐢🐢🐢🐢🐢🐢

A.   Directions: Fill in the blank.

1.   My *friend* is a common noun.   There are many _____in the

world. My friend's name is _____. I am naming a specific

friend; this is a proper noun.

2.   A store is a common noun. There are many _____in the

world.   The name of a specific store is a proper noun. The name of a

store that I know is _____.

🐢🐢🐢🐢🐢🐢🐢🐢🐢🐢🐢🐢🐢🐢🐢🐢🐢🐢

B.   Directions: Circle the proper noun.

1.	boy	Franco	5.	leader	Abraham Lincoln
2.	river	Hudson River	6.	Miami	city
3.	country	Mexico	7.	dam	Hoover Dam
4.	Bambi	deer	8.	Judson School	school

A **common noun** does not name a specific person, place, or thing.

Most nouns are common and are not capitalized.

      Examples: doll   glass

If a type of noun is given, it is still common.   *Example:* horse   pinto

A **proper noun** names a **specific** person, place, or thing. **Capitalize** a proper noun.

    Example: <u>town</u> - <u>Crossville</u>
                 common   proper
                  noun   noun

🐢 🐢 🐢 🐢 🐢 🐢 🐢 🐢 🐢 🐢 🐢 🐢 🐢 🐢 🐢 🐢 🐢 🐢

Directions: Write a **proper noun** on the line.

   Example: The name of a bridge near my town is<u> **White Run Bridge** </u>.

1.   A person I like is _____.

2.   The name of my town (city) is _____.

3.   The name of a street or road in my town is _____.

4.   The name of a store in my town is _____.

5.   The name of a restaurant I like is _____.

6.   I live in the state of _____.

7.   The name of my country is _____.   91

Most nouns are <u>concrete</u> nouns. That means you can see them.

Read this sentence. How many things can be seen?

The boy drives a car down the road.

Can you see a boy? Yes, <u>boy</u> is a noun.

Can you see a car? Yes, <u>car</u> is a noun.

Can you see a road? Yes, <u>road</u> is a noun.

Directions: Circle any nouns.

1. Dad likes cereal and milk.

2. My sister drives a truck.

3. Mrs. Jones walks to the store.

4. A ladder is leaning against the house.

5. The fork and knife just fell on the floor.

6. A turtle and an owl live in our backyard.

7. Mom put sheets and a blanket on that bed.

8. A football and baseball are in the closet.

92

Name_____

Date_____

Most nouns are <u>concrete</u> nouns. That means you can see them.

Read this sentence. How many things can be seen?

Mary put icing on the cake.

Can you see Mary? Yes, <u>Mary</u> is a noun.

Can you see icing? Yes, <u>icing</u> is a noun.

Can you see a cake? Yes, <u>cake</u> is a noun.

🐢 🐢 🐢 🐢 🐢 🐢 🐢 🐢 🐢 🐢 🐢 🐢 🐢 🐢 🐢 🐢 🐢 🐢 🐢

Directions: Circle any nouns.

1.   That flower has lost its petals.

2.   My grandfather buys many books.

3.   Your new shirt is in this bag.

4.   A bowl of cherries is on the table.

5.   Jan and her brother washed their car.

6.   The gift with a red bow is for my mother.

7.   Several nails are lying on the floor by the television.

8.   Mr. Jacobs likes to eat chips with his sandwiches.

Name_____

Date_____

Singular means one.
Plural means more than one.

<u>Singular</u>   <u>Plural</u>
skunk   skunks
grape   grapes
dish   dishes
child   children

Directions: Write **S** if the noun is singular (one) and **P** if the noun is
              plural (more than one).

1. _____ comb   10. _____ watches

2. _____ songs   11. _____ pennies

3. _____ bottle   12. _____ lamp

4. _____ powder   13. _____ goose

5. _____ ears   14. _____ geese

6. _____ lion   15. _____ stamps

7. _____ tooth   16. _____ calves

8. _____ apples   17. _____ pear

9. _____ rug   18. _____ men

NOUNS
Singular and Plural

Singular means one.
Plural means more than one.

🐢 To form the plural of most nouns, add <u>s</u>.

🐢 If a word ends in <u>ch</u>, <u>sh</u>, <u>s</u>, <u>z</u>, or <u>x</u>, add <u>es</u> to form the plural.

Use a dictionary to check the plural form. If <u>es</u> should be added to a noun, it will say, **pl. es.** <u>If no plural (pl.) is given, you know to simply add **s**.</u>

🐢 🐢 🐢 🐢 🐢 🐢 🐢 🐢 🐢 🐢 🐢 🐢 🐢 🐢 🐢 🐢

Directions: Write the plural.

1. star - _____

2. wish - _____

3. dime - _____

4. rock - _____

5. box - _____

6. car - _____

7. bush - _____

8. fizz - _____

9. juice - _____

10. lunch - _____

11. club - _____

12. mix - _____

13. light - _____

14. bus - _____

15. spoon - _____

16. catch - _____

17. bone - _____

18. loss - _____

Singular means one.
Plural means more than one.

🐢 To form the plural of a noun ending in <u>ay</u>, <u>ey</u>, <u>oy</u>, or <u>uy</u>, add **s**. As you know, <u>a</u>, <u>e</u>, <u>i</u>, <u>o</u>, and <u>u</u> are vowels. If a word ends in <u>a, e, i, o</u>, or <u>u</u> **+ y**, add **s**.

Examples:	<u>singular</u>	<u>plural</u>
	bay	bays
	key	keys
	boy	boys
	buy	buys

🐢 To form the plural of a noun ending in a **consonant + y**, change the **y** to <u>i</u> and add **es**.

Examples:	penny	pennies
	lily	lilies

Use a dictionary to check the plural form. If the <u>y</u> should be changed to <u>i</u> and **es** added to a noun, it will say, **pl. *ies*.** <u>If no plural (pl.) is given, you know to simply add **s**.</u>

🐢 🐢 🐢 🐢 🐢 🐢 🐢 🐢 🐢 🐢 🐢 🐢 🐢 🐢 🐢 🐢 🐢 🐢 🐢 🐢

Directions: Write the plural.

1. baby - _____   5. buggy - _____

2. monkey - _____   6. toy - _____

3. lady - _____   7. bunny - _____

4. guy - _____   8. ray - _____

Name_____

Date_____

Singular means one.
Plural means more than one.

🐢 To form the plural of a noun ending in <u>ay</u>, <u>ey</u>, <u>oy</u>, or <u>uy</u>, add <u>**s**</u>. As you know, <u>a</u>, <u>e</u>, <u>i</u>, <u>o</u>, and <u>u</u> are vowels. If a word ends in <u>a</u>, <u>e</u>, <u>i</u>, <u>o</u>, or <u>u</u> **+ <u>y</u>**, add <u>**s**</u>.

Example: monk**ey**   monk**eys**

🐢 To form the plural of a noun ending in a **consonant + <u>y</u>**, change the <u>y</u> to <u>i</u> and add <u>**es**</u>.

Example: strawber**ry**   strawber**ries**

Use a dictionary to check the plural form. If the <u>y</u> should be changed to <u>i</u> and <u>es</u> added to a noun, it will say, **pl. *ies.*** <u>If no plural (pl.) is given, you know to simply add *s*.</u>

🐢 🐢 🐢 🐢 🐢 🐢 🐢 🐢 🐢 🐢 🐢 🐢 🐢 🐢 🐢 🐢 🐢 🐢 🐢

Directions: Write the plural.

1. pony - _____

2. day - _____

3. filly - _____

4. donkey - _____

5. joy - _____

6. berry - _____

7. dummy - _____

8. buy - _____

9. pansy - _____

10. ruby - _____

11. stray - _____

12. mommy - _____

Singular means one.
Plural means more than one.

🐢 To form the plural of some nouns ending in f, change the f to v and add
es.

Examples: **calf - cal<u>ves</u>**
             leaf - lea<u>ves</u>
             loaf - loa<u>ves</u>
             dwarf - dwar<u>ves</u>

🐢 To form the plural of some nouns ending in f, simply add **s**.

Examples: puff - puff**s**
             roof - roof**s**
             belief - belief**s**

Use a dictionary to check the plural form. If the f should be changed to v
and **es** added to a noun such as *calf,* it will say, **pl. ves** or ***pl., calves.*** If
no plural (pl.) is given, you know to simply add **s**.

🐢 🐢 🐢 🐢 🐢 🐢 🐢 🐢 🐢 🐢 🐢 🐢 🐢 🐢 🐢 🐢 🐢 🐢

Directions: Write the plural.

1. loaf - _____   5. cuff - _____

2. whiff - _____   6. half - _____

3. leaf - _____   7. staff - _____

4. proof - _____   8. leaf - _____

Singular means one.
Plural means more than one.

🐢 To form the plural of some nouns ending in <u>o</u>, add **s**.

Examples: zoo   -   zoo**s**
             silo   -   silo**s**

🐢 To form the plural of some nouns ending in <u>o</u>, add **es**.

Example: tomato   -   tomato**es**

🐢 Some nouns ending in <u>o</u> will add **s** or **es**.   When two spellings are given, the first one is preferred. Use the first spelling.

Example: **lasso**....pl., *sos, soes*...

This means that more than one lasso can be spelled *lassos* or *lassoes*. Do you see that *sos* is listed first? Therefore, the best spelling of more than one lasso is *lassos*.

Use a dictionary to check the plural form. <u>If no plural (pl.) is given, you know to simply add **s**.</u>

🐢 🐢 🐢 🐢 🐢 🐢 🐢 🐢 🐢 🐢 🐢 🐢 🐢 🐢 🐢 🐢 🐢 🐢

Directions: Write the plural.

1. potato - _____   4. pogo - _____

2. yoyo - _____   5. stereo - _____

3. rodeo - _____   6. domino - _____

99

Name_____

Date_____

Singular means one.
Plural means more than one.

🐢Some nouns do not change to form the plural.

Example: deer   -   deer

Use a dictionary to check the plural form. If the word does not change, the dictionary will say (pl. deer).

deer...*pl.* deer

🐢Some nouns totally change to form the plural.

Example: child   -   child**ren**

Use a dictionary to check the plural form. If the word does change, the dictionary will say the plural.

child...*pl.* children

🐢🐢🐢🐢🐢🐢🐢🐢🐢🐢🐢🐢🐢🐢🐢🐢🐢🐢🐢

Directions: Write the plural.

1. tooth - _____   6. moose - _____

2. sheep - _____   7. foot - _____

3. mouse - _____   8. woman - _____

4. goose - _____   9. trout - _____

5. elk - _____   10. child - _____

100

Possessive nouns show ownership or that something is part of something else.

Examples: Manny's shoes

a pencil's eraser

🐢 To a singular (one) noun, add **'s** to the noun.

Example: horse   -   horse's stall

It does not matter how many items are owned; **'s** is added to the noun.

Examples: Chan**'s** sister
Chan**'s** sisters

🐢 🐢 🐢 🐢 🐢 🐢 🐢 🐢 🐢 🐢 🐢 🐢 🐢 🐢 🐢 🐢 🐢 🐢

Directions: Write the possessive for each noun.

Example: a purse belonging to my mom - __my mom's purse__

1.   a quarter belonging to Yancy - _____

2.   dogs belonging to Jina - _____

3.   a notebook belonging to her brother - _____

4.   a birthday party for Chessa - _____

5.   a van belonging to Grandma - _____

Possessive nouns show ownership or that something is part of something else.

Examples: Mr. Benson's job

sisters' playhouse

🐢 To a plural (more than one) noun that ends in s, add **'** after the **s**.

Example: more than one bird = bird**s**   -   bird**s'** nest

It does not matter how many items are owned; **s'** is added to the noun.

Examples: boys' baseball

boys' baseballs

🐢🐢🐢🐢🐢🐢🐢🐢🐢🐢🐢🐢🐢🐢🐢🐢🐢🐢🐢

Directions: Write the possessive for each noun.

Example: a ball belonging to two girls - __girls' ball__

1.   an apartment shared by three ladies - _____

2.   a room shared by two sisters - _____

3.   a report done by two boys   - _____

4.   the balloons belonging to three clowns - _____

5.   a store belonging to his aunts - _____

6.   cake eaten by all the guests - _____

TO REVIEW:

🐢 To a singular (one) noun, add **'s** to the noun.

> Example: pig - pig's tail

🐢 To a plural (more than one) noun that ends in s, add **'** after the **s**.

> Example: more than one boy = boy**s** - boy**s'** coach

NEW RULE:

🐢 If a noun is **plural** (more than one) and **does not end in s**, place an apostrophe**(') + s** at the end of the word.

> Example: more than one child = **children** - children**'s** sand box

🐢 🐢 🐢 🐢 🐢 🐢 🐢 🐢 🐢 🐢 🐢 🐢 🐢 🐢 🐢 🐢 🐢 🐢

Directions: Write the possessive for each noun.

1. (review) cheese belonging to a mouse - _____

2. (review) tickets belonging to a woman - _____

3. (review) a dog owned by two friends - _____

4. a box belonging to more than one mouse - _____

5. an office shared by more than one woman - _____

6. a restroom belonging to more than one man - _____

A. Common and Proper Nouns:

Directions: Circle the proper noun.

1. girl   Ellen   3. town   Littlestown

2. Pacific Ocean   ocean   4. creek   Potts Creek

B. Identifying Nouns:

Directions: Circle any nouns.

1. Two horses pulled a wagon.

2. Jan likes chicken with noodles.

3. Several friends met in the cafeteria.

C. Singular and Plural Nouns:

Directions: Write <u>S</u> if the noun is singular; write <u>P</u> if the noun is plural.

Remember: Singular means only one.
Plural means more than one.

1. _____ pan

2. _____ crackers

3. _____ potato

4. _____ blisters

D. Plural Nouns:

Directions: Write the plural of each noun.

1. floor - _____

7. city - _____

2. tomato - _____

8. watch - _____

3. calf -_____

9. boy - _____

4. dairy - _____

10. box - _____

5. deer - _____

11. child - _____

6. flash -_____

12. roof - _____

E. Possessive Nouns:

Directions: Write the possessive.

1. a coat belonging to Jim - _____

2. socks belonging to her brother - _____

3. a ball shared by two friends - _____

4. the workroom for teachers - _____

5. a theater for more than one child - _____

Name_____

Date_____

A.   List of Prepositions:
    Directions: List the twenty-eight prepositions that you have learned.

1. _____   15. _____

2. _____   16. _____

3. _____   17. _____

4. _____   18. _____

5. _____   19. _____

6. _____   20. _____

7. _____   21. _____

8. _____   22. _____

9. _____   23. _____

10. _____   24. _____

11. _____   25. _____

12. _____   26. _____

13. _____   27. _____

14. _____   28. _____

B. Compound Subject:

Directions: Cross out the prepositional phrase in each sentence.
Then, underline the compound subject once and the verb
twice.

Remember: The subject will not be a word in a prepositional phrase.

1. Judy and her brother go to a cabin.

2. Their bikes and skates are in the garage.

C. Compound Verb:

Directions: Cross out the prepositional phrase in each sentence.
Then, underline the subject once and the compound verb
twice.

Remember: The verb will never be a word in a prepositional phrase.

1. Mom sang and danced around the kitchen.

2. His sister looked into the bag and laughed.

D. Imperative Sentence:

Directions: Cross out the prepositional phrase in each sentence.
Then, underline the subject once and the verb twice.

Remember: An imperative sentence gives a command.

1. Keep this in your room.

2. Wait for a few minutes.

E. Contractions:

Directions: Write the contraction in the space provided.

1. we are - _____   4. they are - _____

2. I have - _____   5. you will - _____

3. will not - _____   6. had not - _____

F. It's/Its   They're/There/Their   You're/Your:

Directions: Circle the correct word.

1.   (It's, Its) snowing.

2.   (You're, Your) supposed to be polite.

3.   (They're, There, Their) brother is fishing today.

4.   (They're, There, Their) helping to build a tree house.

G. Can/May:

Directions: Circle the correct word.

1.   (Can, May) you hold this?

2.   (Can, May) we sit with you?

3.   Harry (can, may) hop on one foot.

H.   State of Being:

Directions: Use *is*, *am*, *are*, *was*, or *were* to fill in the blanks.

Present: 1.   I _____ tired.

2.   Today _____ cloudy.

3.   Those children _____ funny.

Past: 1.   Gail _____ afraid of the snake.

2.   Both boys _____ in the pool.

I.   Helping (Auxiliary) Verbs:

Directions: List the twenty-three helping verbs.

d_____   h_____   m_____   c_____   c_____   i____   w_____

d_____   h_____   m_____   sh____   sh____   a____   b_____

d_____   h_____   m_____   w_____   w_____   a____   b_____

                                                          w____   b_____

J. Action?:

Directions: Write <u>Yes</u> if the boldfaced verb shows action. Write <u>No</u> if the boldfaced verb does not show action.

1.   _____   Kenny **pitched** a ball.

2.   _____   She **tasted** the stew.

3.   _____   The stew **tastes** good.   109

K.   Regular or Irregular:

   Directions: Write the past and past participle in the blank. Then, answer the question.

1.   (to paint)   Yesterday, they _____ a house.

   They have _____ two houses on this street.

   To paint is a regular verb if you added *ed.* Is *to paint* a regular or an irregular verb? _____

2.   (to write)   Yesterday, I _____ a letter.

   Glen has _____ his name on his baseball.

   To write is a regular verb if you added *ed.* Is *to write* a regular or an irregular verb? _____

L. Irregular Verbs:

   Directions: Cross out any prepositional phrase(s). Underline the subject once and the verb or verb phrase twice.

1.   Larry had (ate, eaten) earlier.

2.   Sharon may have (went, gone) with her family.

3.   Water was (froze, frozen) in the bucket.

4.   The king has (fallen, fell) off his horse.

5.   Have you ever (rode, ridden) on a city bus?

110

M. Tenses:

Directions: Write the tense of the boldfaced verb.

Remember: The tenses are *present*, *past*, and *future*.

1. _____   Janet **walked** past me.

2. _____   I **shall leave** soon.

3. _____   Scott **loves** to eat.

4. _____   That baby **smiled** at us.

5. _____   Tara and Kent **will stay** home.

N. Subject/Verb Agreement:

Directions: Circle the correct verb.

1. Her aunt (make, makes) dolls.

2. That lamp (shine, shines) too brightly.

3. Misty and her dad (rides, ride) bikes together.

4. Several men (meet, meets) for breakfast.

5. Everyone (is, are) very friendly.

6. One of their friends (collect, collects) stamps.

Name_____ **ADJECTIVES**

Date_____

Most adjectives are describing words.

A red ball is on the long table.

First, find the things you can see in the sentence. These are nouns.
You can see a ball and a table.

Is there a word that describes ball?   **RED** ball

Is there a word that describes table?   **LONG** table

Red and *long* are adjectives.

🐢 🐢 🐢 🐢 🐢 🐢 🐢 🐢 🐢 🐢 🐢 🐢 🐢 🐢 🐢 🐢 🐢 🐢 🐢

Directions: Write an adjective that can describe each noun.

Example: _____**smart**_____ girl

1. _____ bread   7. _____ soup

2. _____ toy   8. _____ box

3. _____ milk   9. _____ tree

4. _____ house   10. _____ car

5. _____ boy   11. _____ rock

6. _____ friend   12. _____ pencil

Date_____

Most adjectives are describing words.

A large, furry bear lives in that dark cave.

First, find the things you can see in the sentence. These are **nouns**.
You can see a **bear** and a **cave**.

Sometimes, **more than one word** will describe a noun.
Two words describe bear: **large** bear   **furry** bear

Only one word describes cave: **dark** cave

Large, *furry*, and *dark* are **adjectives**.

🐢 🐢 🐢 🐢 🐢 🐢 🐢 🐢 🐢 🐢 🐢 🐢 🐢 🐢 🐢 🐢 🐢 🐢

Directions: Write two adjectives that can describe each noun.

Example: ____**little**____ ____**green**____ bug

1. _____ _____ rabbit

2. _____ _____ flower

3. _____ _____ lady

4. _____ _____ building

5. _____ _____ baby

6. _____ _____ monkey

7. _____ _____ boat

Date_____

Most adjectives are describing words.

Directions: Draw a picture of a forest with at least two animals in it.
            Color your picture.

🐢 🐢 🐢 🐢 🐢 🐢 🐢 🐢 🐢 🐢 🐢 🐢 🐢 🐢 🐢 🐢 🐢 🐢

Directions: On the top lines, write two animals you drew in your forest.
            On the double lines, write adjectives that describe each animal.

_____   _____

=======================   =======================

=======================   =======================

=======================   =======================

=======================   =======================

Name_____

ADJECTIVES
Articles

Date_____

**Articles are special adjectives. *A*, *an*, and *the* are articles.
They do not describe. They are called limiting adjectives.**

Rules for using *a*, *an*, and *the*.

A.   **Use <u>the</u> before words beginning with both vowels and
consonants.**

B.   **Use <u>an</u> before words beginning with a vowel.**

an **a**pple
an **e**gg
an **i**ce cream cone
an **o**strich
an **u**mbrella

C.   **Use <u>a</u> before words beginning with a consonant.**

a dollar   a flag   a zebra

🐢 🐢 🐢 🐢 🐢 🐢 🐢 🐢 🐢 🐢 🐢 🐢 🐢 🐢 🐢 🐢 🐢 🐢 🐢

A.   Directions: Write <u>a</u> or <u>an</u> before each word.

1. _____ arm   5. _____ storm   9. _____ bridge

2. _____ chance   6. _____ elephant   10. _____ inn

3. _____ elk   7. _____ afternoon   11. _____ urn

4. _____ icicle   8. _____ open door   12. _____ shower

B.   Directions: Read each sentence. Circle each article. Then, reread the
sentence and circle any describing adjectives.

1. The doll has glass eyes.

2. An otter is a fast swimmer.

115

Name_____

Date_____

Most adjectives describe. Often, descriptive adjectives tell *what kind.*

> Examples: cherry pie
>
> What kind of pie?   cherry

***A, an,* and *the* are called limiting adjectives.**
Some limiting adjectives tell *how many.*

one icy road   How many?   one

several cereal boxes   How many?   several

NUMBERS can be limiting adjectives that tell *how many.*

Several*, *some*, *many*, *few*, *no*,** and ***any can be limiting adjectives that tell *how many.*

🐢 🐢 🐢 🐢 🐢 🐢 🐢 🐢 🐢 🐢 🐢 🐢 🐢 🐢 🐢 🐢 🐢 🐢 🐢

A.   Directions: Write a number that tells *how many.* The number is an adjective.

> Example: _____**one**_____ bird

1. _____ socks   3. _____ dimes

2. _____ days   4. _____ hours

B.   Directions: Write ***several*, *some*, *many*, *few*, *no*,** or ***any*** on each line. These words that tell *how many* serve as adjectives.

1. _____ dollars   3. _____ money

2. _____ boys   4. _____ people

116

Name_____

Date_____

Most adjectives describe. Often, descriptive adjectives tell *what kind.*

Examples: race car

What kind of car?   race

***A, an,* and *the* are called limiting adjectives.**
Some limiting adjectives tell *how many.*

two shoes   How many?   two

many men   How many?   many

NUMBERS can be limiting adjectives that tell *how many.*

***Several, some, many, few, no,* and *any* can be limiting adjectives that**
tell *how many.*

Directions: Read each sentence. First, circle *a, an,* or *the.* Next, look
for words that tell *how many.* Then, circle any describing
adjectives.

1.   A strong wind blew the palm trees.

2.   The short man sat on an old park bench.

3.   Three big goats crossed a troll bridge.

4.   Several tall candles are on the birthday cake.

5.   Four orange striped balls bounced by me.

6.   Many red roses are growing in a flower garden.   117

Adjectives can make comparisons.

The comparative form compares two items.

Example: big   -   bigger

The pan is big, but the kettle is bigger.

Here, a *pan* and a *kettle* (2 items) are being compared in size.

THERE ARE SEVERAL WAYS TO FORM THE COMPARATIVE:

Add er to most one-syllable adjectives.
small - smaller
This bee is smaller than that bug.

Add er to some two-syllable adjectives.
happy - happier
After the game, Adam was happier than his sister.

Place more (or less) before some two-syllable adjectives.
trusting - more trusting
Our beagle is more trusting than our poodle.

Place more (or less) before adjectives of three or more syllables.
beautiful - more beautiful
Of the two gowns, the satin one is more beautiful.

Some adjectives totally change forms when comparing two items.
good - better   bad - worse
She is a better painter than her brother.

118

Name_____

Date_____

Adjectives can make comparisons.

The comparative form compares two items.

> 🐢 Add <u>er</u> to most one-syllable adjectives.
> *dumb - dumber*

> 🐢 Add <u>er</u> to some two-syllable adjectives.
> *funny - funnier*

> 🐢 Place more (or less) before some two-syllable adjectives.
> *loving - more loving*

> 🐢 Place more (or less) before adjectives of three or more
> syllables.
> *fantastic - more fantastic*

> 🐢 Some adjectives totally change forms when comparing
> two items.
> *good - better*   *bad - worse*

🐢 🐢 🐢 🐢 🐢 🐢 🐢 🐢 🐢 🐢 🐢 🐢 🐢 🐢 🐢 🐢 🐢 🐢

A.   Directions: Write the comparative form (for comparing two items).
     Remember: Use a dictionary if necessary.

1. fast - _____   3. patient - _____

2. tiny - _____   4. bad - _____

B.   Directions: Circle the comparative form.

1. Jill's left foot is (smaller, more small) than her right one.

2. The gray kitten is (energeticer, more energetic) than the white one.

3. She's (upseter, more upset) about losing her ring than her keys.

Adjectives can make comparisons.

The superlative form compares three or more items.

Example: tall   -   tallest

Of the three girls, Molly is tallest.

Molly and two other girls are being compared.

THERE ARE SEVERAL WAYS TO FORM THE SUPERLATIVE:

🐢 **Add est to most one-syllable adjectives.**

long - longest

Of the four tables, the wooden one is longest.

🐢 **Add est to some two-syllable adjectives.**

pretty - prettiest

This is the prettiest dress in the store.

🐢 **Place most (or least) before some two-syllable adjectives.**

patient - most patient

Mrs. Kent is the most patient person I know.

🐢 **Place most (or least) before adjectives of three or more syllables.**

delicious - most delicious

All of the pies are delicious, but your apple pie is most delicious.

🐢 **Some adjectives totally change forms when comparing three or more items.**

good - best   bad - worst

"I am the worst speller in our family," said Anne.

120

Name_____

Date_____

Adjectives can make comparisons.

The superlative form compares three or more items.

🐢 **Add <u>est</u> to most one-syllable adjectives.**
dumb - dumbest

🐢 **Add <u>est</u> to some two-syllable adjectives.**
funny - funniest

🐢 **Place most (or least) before some two-syllable adjectives.**
loving - most loving

🐢 **Place most (or least) before adjectives of three or more syllables.**
fantastic - most fantastic

🐢 **Some adjectives totally change forms when comparing two items.**
good - best   *bad - worst*

🐢🐢🐢🐢🐢🐢🐢🐢🐢🐢🐢🐢🐢🐢🐢🐢🐢🐢🐢

A. Directions: Write the superlative form (for comparing three or more items). **Remember: Use a dictionary if necessary.**

1. kind - _____   3. timid - _____

2. quiet - _____   4. brilliant - _____

B. Directions: Circle the comparative form.

1. Of the triplets, Jana is the (hardest, most hard) worker.

2. When Scott told four jokes, his last one was (funniest, most funny).

3. The runner's fifth jump was (perfectest, most perfect).

4. Of the three teachers, Miss Henry is (understandingest, most understanding).

121

Name_____ **ADJECTIVES**

Date_____

The comparative form compares two items.

🐢 **Add er to most one-syllable adjectives.** (tough - tougher)

🐢 **Add er to some two-syllable adjectives.** (icy - icier)

🐢 **Place more (or less) before some two-syllable adjectives.**
   (unkind - more unkind)

🐢 **Place more (or less) before adjectives of three or more syllables.** (different - more different)

🐢 **Some adjectives totally change forms when comparing two items.** (good - better   bad - worse)

The superlative form compares three or more items.

🐢 **Add est to most one-syllable adjectives.** (tough - toughest)

🐢 **Add est to some two-syllable adjectives.** (icy - iciest)

🐢 **Place most (or least) before some two-syllable adjectives.**
   (unkind - most unkind)

🐢 **Place most (or least) before adjectives of three or more syllables.** (different - most different)

🐢 **Some adjectives totally change forms when comparing two items.** (good - best   bad - worst)

🐢🐢🐢🐢🐢🐢🐢🐢🐢🐢🐢🐢🐢🐢🐢🐢🐢🐢

Directions: Circle the correct adjective form.

1. Our first roller coaster ride was (shorter, shortest) than our second one.

2. Clint is the (quieter, quietest) member of his family.

3. Her serve is (more powerful, most powerful) than her backhand.

4. Of all the dogs in the show, Troubles was the (noisier, noisiest).

122

**ADJECTIVES
Review**

A. Describing Words:

Directions: Write two describing words for each noun.

1.   _____   _____   mouse

2.   _____   _____   van

3.   _____   _____   banana

B. A, An, and The:

Directions: Write *a* or *an* before each word or group of words.

1.   _____ bottle   4.   _____ end

2.   _____ ant   5.   _____ organ

3.   _____ grocery store   6.   _____ ice cream sundae

C. Limiting Adjectives:

Directions: Fill in the blank.

1.   The articles that are always adjectives are _____, _____, and _____.

2.   Write an example of a number used as an adjective: _____ pennies.

3.   Write adjectives that tell how many:

   s e _ _ _ _ _   s o _ _   m _ _ _   f _ _   a _ _   n _

D. Identifying Adjectives:

    Directions: Circle each adjective.

Remember: *A*, *an*, and *the* are adjectives.

               Numbers and words like *some*, *several*, *few*, *many*, *no*, and *any* can be limiting adjectives.

       Most adjectives are describing words.

1. Rex looked at a gold watch.

2. The old car has two flat tires.

3. She likes peach pie with whipped cream.

4. Several little puppies slept in an orange basket.

5. Some kittens have blue eyes and soft whiskers.

E. Degrees of Adjectives:

    Directions: Circle the correct form.

1. Mike's new bike is (bigger, biggest) than his old one.

2. This pink mattress is (firmer, more firm) that the blue one.

3. My aunt is (more athletic, most athletic) than my mother.

4. Janell chose the (more colorful, most colorful) blouse on the rack.

5. Of the two coats, the short one has the (better, best) price.

Name_____ **Cumulative Review**
Adjectives

Date_____

A. List of Prepositions:

Directions: List the twenty-eight prepositions that you have learned.

1. a b _ _ _   15. f_ _ _

2. a c _ _ _ _   16. i_

3. a f _ _ _   17. i n _ _ _ _

4. a r _ _ _ _   18. i n _ _

5. a_   19. o_

6. b e _ _ _ _   20. o_ _

7. b e _ _ _ _   21. o_

8. b e _ _ _   22. o_ _

9. b e _ _ _ _   23. o _ _ _

10. b e _ _ _ _ _   24. t h _ _ _ _ _

11. b_   25. t_

12. d_ _ _   26. u_ _ _ _

13. d u _ _ _ _   27. u_

14. f_ _   28. w_ _ _

125

B. Compound Subject and Compound Verb:

   Directions: Cross out the prepositional phrase in each sentence.
                 Then, underline the subject once and the verb twice.

Remember: **The subject or verb will not be a word in a prepositional phrase.**

1.   Craig and his mother went to the beach.

2.   Hannah lay in a chair and read a magazine.

C. Imperative Sentence:

   Directions: Cross out the prepositional phrase in each sentence.
                 Then, underline the subject once and the verb twice.

Remember: **An imperative sentence gives a command.**

1.   Hang this on the wall.

2.   After lunch, meet me by that tree.

D. It's/Its   They're/There/Their   You're/Your:

   Directions: Circle the correct word.

1.   (It's, Its) two o'clock.

2.   (They're, There, Their) are five fish in this bowl.

3.   Do you know if (you're, your) in the next race?

4.   (They're, There, Their) writing a letter to a pen pal.

126

E. Can/May:

Directions: Circle the correct word.

1. (Can, May) I be excused?

2. (Can, May) you untie this for me?

3. She (can, may) be arriving soon.

F. Contractions:

Directions: Write the contraction in the space provided.

1. I will - _____

2. who is - _____

3. cannot - _____

4. here is - _____

5. you are - _____

6. there is - _____

7. it is- _____

8. they will - _____

9. I am - _____

10. is not - _____

11. they are - _____

12. are not - _____

13. will not - _____

14. what is - _____

15. they will - _____

16. do not - _____

17. what is - _____

18. we are - _____

G.   State of Being:

   Directions: Underline the subject once and the verb twice. Label the
                 direct object - **D.O.**

Remember: **The direct object receives the action of the verb.**

                                D.O.
   Example: Her <u>mom</u> <u><u>paints</u></u> cars.   The **object** her mom paints is *cars.*

1.   She packs her lunch.

2.   Gary blew bubbles.

3.   The doorman opened the door.

H.   Helping (Auxiliary) Verbs:

   Directions: List the twenty-three helping verbs.

d_____   h_____   m_____   c_____   c_____   i____   w_____

d_____   h_____   m_____   sh____   sh____   a____   b_____

d_____   h_____   m_____   w_____   w_____   a____   b_____

                                                       w____   b_____

I.   Action?:

   Directions: Write <u>Yes</u> if the boldfaced verb shows action. Write <u>No</u> if
                 the boldfaced verb does not show action.

1.   _____   Miss Land **handed** me a pencil.

2.   _____   Mom **looked** at her shopping list.

3.   _____   This shirt **looks** dirty.

J. Regular or Irregular:

Directions: Write the past and past participle in the blank. Then, answer the question.

Review: (to jump) Yesterday, we _____rope.

I had _____ ten minutes before missing.

To jump is a regular verb if you added *ed.* Is *to jump* a regular or an irregular verb? _____

Directions: Write <u>RV</u> in the blank if the verb is regular. Write <u>IV</u> if the verb is irregular.

1. _____ to slap   3. _____ to break   5. _____ to cry

2. _____ to ride   4. _____ to ring   6. _____ to sit

K. Irregular Verbs:

Directions: Cross out any prepositional phrase(s). Underline the subject once and the verb or verb phrase twice.

1. Our balloons have (burst, busted).

2. Max may have (went, gone) with his grandpa.

3. Mrs. Gant must have (written, wrote) to the mayor.

4. You should have (did, done) your homework before dinner.

5. Has Millie ever (gave, given) you a birthday card?

L. Tenses:

Directions: Write the tense of the boldfaced verb.
Remember: The tenses are *present*, *past*, and *future*.

1. _____   Tonight, I **shall bake** cookies.

2. _____   A bell **rang**.

3. _____   Connie **rides** her horse every day.

4. _____   The workers **poured** concrete.

M.   Subject/Verb Agreement:

Directions: Circle the correct verb.

1. I (like, likes) to play games.

2. Some flowers (open, opens) only during the day.

3. Pam and her friend (draws, draw) cartoons.

4. Each of your buttons (is, are) missing.

N.   Common and Proper Noun:

Directions: Write a proper noun for each common noun.

1. lake -_____   3. state -_____

2. person -_____   4. store - _____

130

O. Common or Proper Nouns:

Directions: Write <u>C</u> if the noun is common. Write <u>P</u> if the noun is proper.

1. _____ BIRD   3. _____ COUNTRY   5. _____ VAN

2. _____ PARROT   4. _____ AMERICA   6. _____ UTAH

P. Singular and Plural Nouns:

Directions: Write the plural.

1. latch - _____   10. curb - _____

2. name - _____   11. box - _____

3. dish - _____   12. gulf - _____

4. glass - _____   13. deer - _____

5. mouse - _____   14. ox - _____

6. potato - _____   15. child - _____

7. goose - _____   16. flea - _____

8. story - _____   17. play - _____

9. calf - _____   18. moose - _____

Q.   Possessive Nouns:

Directions: Write the possessive.

1.   a pet belonging to Kyle - _____

2.   cats belonging to Mr. Bond - _____

3.   a ball shared by four girls - _____

4.   a hotel room shared by more than one woman - _____

R.   Noun Identification:

Directions: Circle any nouns.

**Remember: A noun names a person, place, or thing.
               Look for "things" you can see.**

1.   Three cows stood by an old fence.

2.   Bob and his dad run in the park.

3.   Karen put bread into the toaster.

4.   Your ring and bracelet are on the chair.

5.   A basket of strawberries is by our front door.

Date_____

And, **but**, and **or** usually join two or more other words. They are called **conjunctions**.

> Examples: Ed **and** Tim are brothers.
>
>   Do you want mashed potatoes **or** a baked potato?
>
>   I like carrots **but** not celery.

🐢 🐢 🐢 🐢 🐢 🐢 🐢 🐢 🐢 🐢 🐢 🐢 🐢 🐢 🐢 🐢 🐢 🐢 🐢

A.   Directions: Write <u>**and**</u> on the dotted lines and fill in the blank.

1. pizza **a** _ _ _____

2. bacon **a** _ _ _____

3. up **a** _ _ _____

4. in **a** _ _ _____

5. knife, fork, **a** _ _ _____

6. eyes, nose, **a** _ _ _____

B.   Fill in the blank with <u>**or**</u> or <u>**but**</u>.

1. You may stay _____ leave.

2. She cut her leg, _____ it's healing.

3. He wants tea _____ coffee.

4. I'll wait, _____ you must hurry.

133

Date_____

Words that express emotion are called interjections.

      Examples: Yippee! I'm the winner!

                  Wow! My new bike is great!

Sometimes, interjections will have two or more words.

      Examples: Oh no! I can't believe I did that!

                  Boo hiss! We have to leave!

A special punctuation mark called an exclamation point is placed after an interjection.

🐢 🐢 🐢 🐢 🐢 🐢 🐢 🐢 🐢 🐢 🐢 🐢 🐢 🐢 🐢 🐢 🐢 🐢

A. Directions: Write an interjection and an exclamation point on the line provided.

1. _____ George caught the ball!

2. _____ Dad is buying us ice cream cones!

3. _____ We won!

B. Directions: Circle any interjection.

1. Drats! I'm not allowed to go!

2. This milk is sour! Yuck!

3. Yikes! Look out!

4. Hurrah! Our team beat the Redbirds!

134

🐢 **Adverbs can tell how someone does or did something.**
    Justin swung the bat smoothly.

someone	**did**	**how**
Justin	swung	smoothly

Swung is the verb.   **Smoothly** tells *how* Justin swung the bat.

🐢 **Adverbs can tell how something does (did) something.**
    The kite dips quickly in the wind.

something	**did**	**how**
kite	dips	quickly

Dips is the verb.   **Quickly** tells *how* the kite dips in the wind.

Most adverbs that tell *how* go over to (modify) a verb and end in <u>ly</u>. However, some do not. *Fast, hard,* and *well* tell *how* and do not end in <u>ly</u>.

🐢 🐢 🐢 🐢 🐢 🐢 🐢 🐢 🐢 🐢 🐢 🐢 🐢 🐢 🐢 🐢 🐢 🐢 🐢

A. Directions: Write a word that tells *how*. That word is an adverb.

1. He sings _____.   4. A bird chirped _____.

2. They played _____.   5. She runs _____.

3. I sneezed _____.   6. The wind blew _____.

B. Directions: Write a verb before the boldfaced adverb.

1. The drummer _____ **loudly.**

2. The man and woman _____ **angrily.**

3. Vonnie _____ **happily.**

Name_____   **ADVERBS**
                                        How?
Date_____

🐢 **Adverbs can tell *how*.**

A. Directions: Fill in the blank.

      Example: The girls played jacks quietly.

             Quietly tells _____**how**_____ the girls __**played jacks**___.

1. Susan answered calmly.

    Calmly tells _____ Susan _____.

2. Water tumbled swiftly over rocks.

    Swiftly tells _____ the water _____.

3. Dick yells loudly for his team.

    Loudly tells _____ Dick _____.

4. They cleaned their room well.

    Well tells _____ they _____.

B. Directions: Circle the adverb in each sentence. Then, draw a line to the verb it goes over to (modifies).

Note: Crossing out prepositional phrases will help you. An adverb that tells *how* will not usually be in a prepositional phrase.

1. The winner smiled cheerfully at us.

2. She sat on the old chair carefully.

3. A car slid dangerously around the curve.

136

Name_____   **ADVERBS**
                                         How?
Date_____

🐢 **An adjective, as you have learned, describes a noun.**

     Jim is a **loud** drummer.

       Loud is an adjective that describes drummer.

🐢 The adverb form of <u>loud</u> is **loudly**. <u>Loudly</u> tells *how* Jim plays.

     Incorrect: Jim plays the drums loud.
       Correct: Jim plays the drums **loudly**.

ADJECTIVE	**ADVERB**
slow	slowly
kind	kindly
angry	angrily

🐢 🐢 🐢 🐢 🐢 🐢 🐢 🐢 🐢 🐢 🐢 🐢 🐢 🐢 🐢 🐢 🐢 🐢 🐢

A.   Directions: Write the adverb form of each adjective:

1. quick - _____   4. shy - _____

2. careless - _____   5. hopeful - _____

3. firm - _____   6. tight - _____

B.   Directions: Write the adverb form of the adjective in parenthesis ( ).

1. (playful)   The kitten chased the ball of yarn _____.

2. (polite)   We always answer _____.

3. (loose)   His shirt fits _____.

4. (neat)   Val folds towels _____.

5. (cautious)   The driver approached the light _____.

ADVERBS
How?

It is important to use the correct adverb form in our speaking and writing.

ADJECTIVE	**ADVERB**
slow	slowly

The following sentence is incorrect: **I talk slow.**

I am a slow talker. *Slow* describes talker.

Slow is an adjective. *Slow* cannot tell how I talk.

Correct: I talk slowly.

However, there are several words that are the same in both adjective and adverb forms:

Examples:
     adjective   adverb
     Ken is a **fast** runner.   He runs **fast**.
     adjective   adverb
     Lori is a **hard** hitter.   She hits **hard**.

Directions: Write the adverb form of each adjective.

1.   (light)   The nurse pressed _____ on the man's arm.

2.   (fast)   That trains travels _____.

3.   (tearful)   The child answered _____.

4.   (hard)   Rick slammed the door too _____.

5.   (bright)   The sun shines _____.

6.   (serious)   Her father spoke _____ about the accident.

138

🐢 **Adverbs can tell when something happens (happened).**

Example: Yesterday, Julia fished for two hours.

Yesterday tells when Julia fished.

Most adverbs that tell *when* **go over to (modify) a verb.**

Some adverbs that tell *when* are:

now	**late**	**always**	**sometimes**	**yesterday**
then	**later**	**never**	**early**	**today**
soon	**when**	**forever**	**earlier**	**tomorrow**
sooner	**first**	**again**	**daily**	**tonight**

There are others. Simply decide if any word in the sentence tells *when.*

🐢 🐢 🐢 🐢 🐢 🐢 🐢 🐢 🐢 🐢 🐢 🐢 🐢 🐢 🐢 🐢 🐢 🐢

A.   Directions: Write an adverb that tells *when.*

1.   Shelley _____ swims.

2.   They arrived _____.

3.   Patsy _____ whispers.

4.   _____, I shall stay up late.

5.   You may go _____.

B.   Directions: Write a verb in each sentence.

1.   We are _____ **today**.

2.   May I _____ **soon**?

3.   **When** will you _____? 139

🐢 **Adverbs can tell where.**

Example: Come here.

Here tells *where* you should come.

Most adverbs that tell *where* usually **go over to (modify) a verb**. Some adverbs that tell *where* are:

here	**everywhere**	**in**	**up**
there	**anywhere**	**out**	**down**
where	**somewhere**	**inside**	**around**

There are others. Simply decide if any **word** in the sentence tells *where*.

🐢 🐢 🐢 🐢 🐢 🐢 🐢 🐢 🐢 🐢 🐢 🐢 🐢 🐢 🐢 🐢 🐢 🐢 🐢

A.   Directions: Write an adverb that tells *where.*

1.   Look _____.

2.   Stand _____.

3.   I want to go _____.

4.   Come _____.

5.   Have you searched _____for your money?

B. Directions: Write a verb in each sentence.

1.   They _____ **here.**

2.   William _____**out.**

3. She _____ **down.**

140

🐢 **Adverbs can tell to what extent.**

There are seven adverbs that usually tell *to what extent:* **not, so, very, too, quite, rather,** and **somewhat.**

Examples: She is **not** happy.   This is **quite** good.

I am **so** hot!   It's **rather** windy.

I am **somewhat** sad.   I'm **too** tired.

Her cousin is **very** talented.

There are other words that tell *to what extent.* Look for words such as *unusually* or *extremely*.

🐢 🐢 🐢 🐢 🐢 🐢 🐢 🐢 🐢 🐢 🐢 🐢 🐢 🐢 🐢 🐢 🐢 🐢 🐢

Directions: Circle any adverbs that tell *to what extent.*

1. The dog was not friendly.

2. I am so busy.

3. Her hair is very pretty.

4. This soup is too cold.

5. She is quite sick.

6. This road is rather curvy.

7. I'm somewhat worried.

8. Mrs. Land is extremely funny.

🐢 **Adverbs can make comparisons.**

The comparative form compares **two** things.

Example: *I* run **faster** than my *brother.*

🐢 There are three ways to form the comparative form:
1. Add **er** to most one-syllable adverbs.

fast - faster

2. Add **more** before most two or more syllable adverbs.

cheerfully - more cheerfully

Some two-syllable words add **er**.

early - earlier

Use a dictionary to check if <u>er</u> should be added. **If the dictionary does not say *adv. er*, use <u>more</u>.**

3. Some adverbs totally change form.

well - better

🐢🐢🐢🐢🐢🐢🐢🐢🐢🐢🐢🐢🐢🐢🐢🐢🐢🐢🐢

Directions: Write the correct form of the boldfaced adverb.

1. James talks **fast**.
    However, his sister talks _____.

2. Candy writes **neatly**.
    However, her dad writes _____.

3. They didn't play ball **well** today.
    They played _____ yesterday.

142

🐢 **Adverbs can make comparisons.**

The superlative form compares **three or more** things.

Example: I run fastest of all my friends.

🐢 There are three ways to form the superlative form:
1. Add **est** to most one-syllable adverbs.

fast - fastest

2. Add **most** before most two or more syllable adverbs.

cheerfully - most cheerfully

Some two-syllable words add **est**.

early - earliest

Use a dictionary to check if <u>est</u> should be added. **If the dictionary does not say *adv. est*, use <u>most</u>.**

3. Some adverbs totally change form.

well - best

🐢 🐢 🐢 🐢 🐢 🐢 🐢 🐢 🐢 🐢 🐢 🐢 🐢 🐢 🐢 🐢 🐢 🐢 🐢

Directions: Write the correct form of the boldfaced adverb.

1. Troy throws the ball **high** in the air.
   In fact, on his team, he throws it _____.

2. During her first show, she danced **beautifully**.
   She danced _____ during her third show.

3. Their group did **well** in the finals.
   They did _____ during the sixth game.

143

🐢 **The comparative form compares *two* things.**

    1.   Add **er** to most one-syllable adverbs.

    2.   Add **more** before most two or more syllable adverbs.

         However, some two-syllable words add **er**.

    3.   Some adverbs totally change form.

🐢 **The superlative form compares *three or more* things.**

    1.   Add **est** to most one-syllable adverbs.

    2.   Add **most** before most two or more syllable adverbs.

         However, some two-syllable words add **est**.

    3.   Some adverbs totally change form.

🐢🐢🐢🐢🐢🐢🐢🐢🐢🐢🐢🐢🐢🐢🐢🐢🐢🐢🐢

Directions: Circle the correct form.

1.   This red toy car goes (faster, fastest) than the white one.

2.   Alice works (more cheerfully, most cheerfully) than her friend.

3.   Kermie tried (harder, hardest) on his third try.

4.   The children sang (better, best) during their second performance.

5.   I did my second lesson (more carefully, most carefully) than my first.

6.   Barbara pitched the ball (harder, hardest) the third time.

7.   Is Venus (closer, closest) of all the planets?

8.   Her truck runs (more smoothly, most smoothly) than our car.

Name_____

Date_____

No, **not (n't)**, **never**, **none**, **nobody**, and **nothing** are negative words.

Do not use more than one negative word in the same sentence.

Example: Wrong: I do**n't** want **nothing**.

Right: I want **nothing**.

or

I do**n't** want anything.

However, if <u>no</u> is used to answer a question, another negative word may be used in the sentence.

Have you found your baseball glove?

No, I have **not** begun to look for it.

🐢 🐢 🐢 🐢 🐢 🐢 🐢 🐢 🐢 🐢 🐢 🐢 🐢 🐢 🐢 🐢 🐢 🐢 🐢

A. Directions: Unscramble these negative words.

1. gintohn - _____   4. oenn - _____

2. reven - _____   5. on - _____

3. otn - _____   6. bdoyon - _____

B. Directions: Circle the correct word.

1. I don't want (none, any).

2. Carl doesn't have (anybody, nobody) with him.

3. They never have (no, any) extra pennies.

4. Jordan cannot drink (anything, nothing) with sugar.

145

Name_____   **ADVERBS**
                                           Review
Date_____

A. Adverbs:

Directions: Write the adverb form of the word.

1. happy - _____   3. wise - _____

2. sweet - _____   4. tearful - _____

B. Adverbs That Tell How:

Directions: Fill in the blank.

1. My dad is a light sleeper.

He sleeps _____.

2. They wrote correct answers.

They answered _____.

3. Karla is a bold speaker.

She spoke _____ against the law.

C. Adverbs That Tell How:

Directions: Circle the adverb that tells *how*.

1. The light shone brightly.

2. Mack can jump high.

3. That dog barks loudly.

4. I erase carefully.

5. We play cards well.

D. Adverbs That Tell When:

Directions: Circle the adverb that tells *when*.

1. He rises earlier on Sunday.

2. Do that again.

3. Sometimes, Ben sleeps in a tent.

4. Linda always writes thank you cards.

5. Let's go to a hockey game tonight.

E. Adverbs That Tell Where:

Directions: Circle the adverb that tells *where*.

1. I can go nowhere today.

2. The man stood up.

3. Where is my ball?

4. The fawn lay down by his mother.

5. Their cousins visit here in June.

F.   Adverbs That Tell to What Extent:

Directions: Circle the adverb that tells *to what extent*.

1. Toby's friend is so serious.

2.   My uncle drives very slowly.

3.   The dog is too large for his doghouse.

4.   Her arms are somewhat burned.

5.   The teacher gave me a rather strange look.

G.   Degrees of Adverbs:

Directions: Circle the correct form.

1.   She speaks English (more plainly, most plainly) than German.

2.   He writes (better, best) with his right hand.

3.   Marie rides her bike (faster, fastest) of all her friends.

4.   Her collie barks (oftener, more often) than her neighbor's poodle.

5.   Shawn glided (more steadily, most steadily) of all the surfers.

Date_____

There are **four** types of sentences.

     A **declarative** sentence makes a <u>statement</u>. It ends in a ***period***.

       This candy bar melted.

     An **interrogative** sentence asks a <u>question</u>. It ends with a ***question mark***.

       Has the candy bar melted?

     An **imperative** sentence gives a <u>command</u>. It ends with a ***period***.

       Give me that candy bar.

     An **exclamatory sentence** <u>shows emotion</u>.   It ends with an ***exclamation point.***

       Yuck! This candy bar is melted!

Directions: Write the sentence type.

1.   Pass the mustard.   _____

2.   May I read your poem?   _____

3.   We passed the test!   _____

4.   Mort got a speeding ticket.   _____

5.   Don't touch that, please.   _____

6.   Her arm was broken in two places.   _____

Date_____

There are **four** types of sentences.

🐢 A **declarative** sentence makes a <u>statement</u>. It ends in a ***period***.

Jodi ate the chips.

🐢 An **interrogative** sentence asks a <u>question</u>. It ends with a ***question mark***.

Has Jodi eaten all the chips?

🐢 An **imperative** sentence gives a <u>command</u>. It ends with a ***period***.

Try these onion chips.

🐢 An **exclamatory sentence** <u>shows emotion</u>.   It ends with an ***exclamation point***.

These chips taste terrible!

🐢 🐢 🐢 🐢 🐢 🐢 🐢 🐢 🐢 🐢 🐢 🐢 🐢 🐢 🐢 🐢 🐢 🐢 🐢 🐢

Directions: Write a sentence for each type.

1.   declarative: _____

2.   interrogative: _____

3.   imperative: _____

4.   exclamatory: _____

Pronouns take the place of nouns.

NOUN	PRONOUN
Tara	she
Marco	he
book	it

Subject pronouns usually serve as the subject of a sentence. These include **I**, **he**, **she**, **we**, **they**, **who**, **you**, and **it**. Subject pronouns are also called nominative pronouns.

Examples: **Kala** likes to camp.
She likes to camp.

Mano and **Van** are friends.
They are friends.

🐢 🐢 🐢 🐢 🐢 🐢 🐢 🐢 🐢 🐢 🐢 🐢 🐢 🐢 🐢 🐢 🐢 🐢 🐢

Directions: In part A, write a person's name. In part B, write a pronoun for the name. In the double underlined part, finish the sentence.

Example: A.   _____**Leah**_____ is my friend.

B.   _____**She**_____ likes _to brush her dogs._

1.   A.   _____ is my friend.

B.   _____ lives _____

2.   A.   My name is _____.

B.   _____ am _____

3.   A.   Two people I know are _____ and _____.

B.   _____ like _____

Pronouns take the place of nouns.

Subject pronouns usually serve as the subject of a sentence. These include

I, **he**, **she**, **we**, **they**, **who**, **you**, and **it**.

> Example: **Hank** has a new bike.
> **He** keeps it in the garage.

Important: If you are talking about yourself, use the pronoun, **I**, at or near
the beginning of the sentence.

> Example: During the storm, **I** stayed inside.

> When referring to yourself and another person, say the other
> person's name first.

> Example: Jean and **I** made cloth dolls.

Do not say Jean and me or me and Jean.

🐢 🐢 🐢 🐢 🐢 🐢 🐢 🐢 🐢 🐢 🐢 🐢 🐢 🐢 🐢 🐢 🐢 🐢 🐢

Directions: On the line provided, write each sentence correctly.

1.   My mom and me like potato chips.

_____

2.   I and my sister play the flute.

_____

3.   Me and my friend want to go to recess.

_____

4.   Their dad and me play catch.

_____

Name_____

Date_____

Pronouns take the place of nouns.

Subject pronouns are **I**, **he**, **she**, **we**, **they**, **who**, **you**, and **it**.

They serve as the subject of a sentence.

Examples: **I** like to play in the sand.

He joined a club.

She braids her hair.

Yesterday, **we** went grocery shopping.

They often watch television.

Who wants ice cream?

You need to earn extra money.

It is 5:00.

🐢 🐢 🐢 🐢 🐢 🐢 🐢 🐢 🐢 🐢 🐢 🐢 🐢 🐢 🐢 🐢 🐢 🐢 🐢

Directions: Circle the correct pronoun.

1.   (We, Us) gave our dog a bath.

2.   May (me, I) play, too?

3.   Yesterday, (they, them) went to a baseball game.

4.   During lunch, (him, he) sits by himself.

5.   (Her, She) laughs often.

6.   Tonight, Bud and (me, I) are going to make dinner.

Object pronouns are **me**, **him**, **her**, **us**, **them**, **whom**, **you**, and **it**.
They can serve as an *object of the preposition*.

🐢 **Remember: An object of the preposition is the word that comes <u>after</u> a preposition.**

Take this *to* your dad.

To is a preposition.

To your dad is a prepositional phrase.

Dad is the last word of the prepositional phrase.

Dad is the <u>object of the preposition</u>.

Use **me**, **him**, **her**, **us**, **them**, **whom**, **you**, or **it** after a preposition.

Example: Jenny went shopping *with* **Dawn**.
Jenny went shopping *with* **her**.

🐢 🐢 🐢 🐢 🐢 🐢 🐢 🐢 🐢 🐢 🐢 🐢 🐢 🐢 🐢 🐢 🐢 🐢

Directions: Place an <u>X</u> above the preposition. Then, circle the correct pronoun.

1.   This present is from (me, I).

2.   You may sit by (we, us).

3.   Uncle Sunny talked to (her, she).

4.   The letter is for (they, them).

5.   Tanya rode bikes with (him, he).

6.   An airplane flew over (us, we).

154

Name_____

Date_____

Object pronouns are **me**, **him**, **her**, **us**, **them**, **whom**, **you**, and **it**.
They can serve as a ***direct object***.

🐢 **Remember:** **A direct object receives the action of the verb.**

The child hit Peter. The **object** the child hit was *Peter*.
The child hit **him** on the leg.

Doris planted a tree. The **object** Doris planted was a tree.
Doris planted **it** last Monday.

Use **me**, **him**, **her**, **us**, **them**, **whom**, **you**, or **it** as a direct object.

Example: Mr. Cline met **Stan** and **Bobby** in Canada.
Mr. Cline met **them** in Canada.

🐢 🐢 🐢 🐢 🐢 🐢 🐢 🐢 🐢 🐢 🐢 🐢 🐢 🐢 🐢 🐢 🐢 🐢

Directions: In part A, underline the subject once and the verb twice.
Label the direct object - <u>D.O.</u> In part B, write a pronoun for the
word labeled as a direct object.

1. A. Rob sees Eileen often.

   B. Rob sees _____ often.

2. A. Micah pushed Todd down.

   B. Micah pushed _____ down.

3. A. The customer dropped a quarter.

   B. The customer dropped _____.

4. A. Everyone likes _____. (Write your name in the blank.)

   B. Everyone likes _____.

🐢 **Sometimes, there is more than one subject in a sentence.**

Example: **Gregg** and **Annie** built a fort.

🐢 **Sometimes, there is more than one object.**

Example: The teacher walked with **Susie** and **Lance**.

PRONOUN FINGER TRICK:

If you are unsure which pronoun to use, place your finger(s) over the **first part** of the compound. Usually, the pronoun that sounds right is correct.

Example: Gregg and (she, her) built a fort.

___She___ built a fort.

Gregg and (her, **she**) built a fort.

Example: The teacher walked with Susie and (he, him).

The teacher walked with ___him___.

The teacher walked with Susie and (he, **him**).

🐢 🐢 🐢 🐢 🐢 🐢 🐢 🐢 🐢 🐢 🐢 🐢 🐢 🐢 🐢 🐢 🐢 🐢

Directions: Circle the correct pronoun.

Remember: Place your finger(s) over the first part of the compound. Then, reread the sentence and choose the correct pronoun.

1.   Rebecca sits beside Tally and (I, me).

2.   Jay and (I, me) went to the movies.

3.   Mom and (her, she) enjoy bridge.

4.   Has Tracy gone with Chase and (she, him)?

Name_____

Date_____

PRONOUN FINGER TRICK:

If you don't know which pronoun to use, place your finger(s) over the **first part** of the compound. Usually, the pronoun that sounds right is correct.

Examples: They handed awards to Julie and (me, I).
They handed awards to   (**me**, I).

Krista and (we, us) will be in charge.
... (**we**, us) will be in charge.

Directions: Circle the correct pronoun.

Remember: Place your finger(s) over the first part of the compound. Then, reread the sentence and choose the correct pronoun.

1.   Marsha and (I, me) became sick.

2.   The thief was looking at their luggage and (they, them).

3.   Sit behind Randy and (me, I).

4.   A bee buzzed around our dad and (we, us).

5.   Miss Stump and (he, him) married last spring.

6.   After the final inning, Jamie and (her, she) bought soda.

7.   The flowers are from Mother and (him, he).

8.   Next week, his dad and (them, they) are going to Texas.

Name_____

Date_____

A possessive pronoun takes the place of a noun and shows ownership.

my	**mine**
his	
her	**hers**
your	**yours**
its	
our	**ours**
their	**theirs**

My, his, her, your, its, our, and *their* will come **before** a noun (or pronoun).
Mine, hers, yours, ours, and *theirs* will come **after** a noun (or pronoun).

Example: shoes belonging to Juan
Juan's shoes
his shoes

🐢 🐢 🐢 🐢 🐢 🐢 🐢 🐢 🐢 🐢 🐢 🐢 🐢 🐢 🐢 🐢 🐢 🐢 🐢
Directions: Write a possessive pronoun on the line.

1.   Craig has black hair, and _____ hair is curly.

2.   Gigi owns a parakeet, but _____ parakeet is not yellow.

3.   Mr. and Mrs. Pod fly to Reno because _____ son lives there.

4.   Ike said, "I like to dive, and _____ favorite spot is Lake Erie."

5.   The lion roared and twitched _____ tail.

6.   Look down. _____ shoelaces are loose.

7.   This is not your book. It is _____.

158

Name_____

Date_____

PRONOUNS
Its, It's
Your, You're
Their, There, They're

🐢 *Its* **is a possessive pronoun.**
> The dog wagged *its* tail.
If you can use *its*, ask *its what?* In this case, *its tail.*

🐢 *Your* **is a possessive pronoun**.
> *Your* dinner is getting cold.
If you can use *your*, ask *your what?* In this case, *your dinner.*

🐢 **Their is a possessive pronoun.**
> *Their* parents are nice.
If you can use *their*, ask *their what?* In this case, *their parents.*

Remember, their is spelled <u>the + ir</u>.
There is an adverb telling where. *They're* is a contraction for *they are.*

🐢 🐢 🐢 🐢 🐢 🐢 🐢 🐢 🐢 🐢 🐢 🐢 🐢 🐢 🐢 🐢 🐢 🐢 🐢

Directions: Circle the correct word.

1.   (Your, You're) very lucky.

2.   Gigi has (your, you're) jacket.

3.   Someone stole (their, they're, there) car.

4.   A purse fell over on (its, it's) side.

5.   (Its, It's) probably true.

6.   I wonder if (their, they're, there) leaving today.

7.   He believes that (your, you're) not feeling well.

8.   Have you ever been (their, they're, there)?

Directions: Circle the correct word.

1.   (Its, It's) a close race.

2.   This salsa is spicy, but (its, it's) not too hot.

3.   The desk is new, yet (its, it's) top looks used.

4.   (Your, You're) peanut butter sandwich is on the counter.

5.   (Your, You're) always so quiet.

6.   Does she know about (your, you're) plans?

7.   (Their, They're, There) making pancakes.

8.   (Their, They're, There) are no pencils in this box.

9.   (Their, They're, There) cousins are from Denver.

10.   An elephant lifted (its, it's) head and trumpeted.

11.   (Your, You're) the only one who can help me.

12.   I like (your, you're) checked wallpaper.

13.   She asked if (their, they're, there) uncle golfs.

14.   He doesn't know if (their, they're, there) leaving tomorrow.

15.   The bank opens (its, it's) doors at nine o'clock.

A. Subject Pronouns:

Subject pronouns usually serve as the subject of a sentence.
Subject pronouns include **I**, **he**, **she**, **we**, **they**, **you**, and **it**.

Directions: In part A, write a person's name. In part B, write a
pronoun for the name. In the double underlined part,
finish the sentence.

Example: A. _____**Les**_____ is a fireman.

B. _____**He**_____ works _in San Diego._

1.   A.   _____ is my principal.

B.   _____ is _____

2.   A.   _____ and I are friends.

B.   _____ like _____

B.   Using I:

Directions: Rewrite the sentence correctly.

1.   My friend and me go to the park.

_____

2.   Me and my dog chase each other.

_____

C.   Object Pronouns - Object of the Preposition:

Object pronouns can serve as an object of the preposition. Object pronouns include **me**, **him**, **her**, **us**, **them**, **you**, and **it**.

Directions: Place an <u>X</u> above the preposition. Then, circle the correct pronoun.

1.   The waiter stared at (she, her).

2.   A stranger walked toward (we, us).

3.   You may enter after (I, me).

4.   A laughing child put a bug on (him, he).

D.   Object Pronouns - Direct Object:

Object pronouns can serve as a direct object. Object pronouns include **me**, **him**, **her**, **us**, **them**, **you**, and **it**.

Directions: In part A, underline the subject once and the verb twice.
Label the direct object - <u>D.O.</u> In part B, write a pronoun for the word labeled as a direct object.

1.   A.   A wasp stung Helen.

    B.   A wasp stung _____.

2.   A.   His remark hurt Allan and his sister.

    B.   His remark hurt _____.

3.   A.   The teacher likes Darla and _____. *(Write your name.)*

    B.   The teacher likes _____.

E. Subject or Object Pronouns:

   Directions: Circle the correct pronoun.

1. Corey slapped (me, I) on the back.

2. No, don't pick (he, him) up!

3. During her break, (she, her) reads.

4. A man reached above (we, us) for his hat.

5. Miss Lane gave directions to (they, them).

6. Do (we, us) need an umbrella today?

F. Compound Pronouns:

   Directions: Circle the correct pronoun.

🐢 **Remember:**   **Place your finger(s) over the first part of the compound. Then, reread the sentence and choose the correct pronoun.**

1. A porter carried bags for our parents and (we, us).

2. The Jensens and (them, they) are having a picnic.

3. Martha and (I, me) rode a pony.

4. Do you want to ride with Nicky and (I, me)?

5. Shannon and (he, him) play bingo.   163

G. Possessive Pronouns:

A possessive pronoun takes the place of a noun and shows ownership.
My (mine), his, her (hers), your (yours), its, our (ours), and **their (theirs)** are possessive pronouns.

Directions: Write a possessive pronoun on the line.

1.   I am having fun, and _____ day is going well.

2.   You need to take _____ dish to the sink.

3.   Several cows lay in the field. _____ calves grazed nearby.

4.   My sister and I made a toy boat, and _____ father painted it.

H.   Its/It's, Your/You're, Their/They're/There:

Directions: Circle the correct word.

1.   (Its, It's) becoming cloudy.

2.   Do I have (your, you're) phone number?

3.   (Their, They're, There) kitten sleeps in a box.

4.   Tomorrow, (their, they're, there) climbing a mountain.

5.   The rat had a string caught in (its, it's) foot.

6.   (Your, You're) the leader of our team.

A.   Prepositions and Verb Phrases:

Directions: Cross out any prepositional phrase(s). Underline the
subject once and the verb or verb phrase twice.

Remember: helping verb(s) + main verb = verb phrase
may have   gone   = may have gone

1.   A stray cat is sitting on our patio.

2.   They must have left before the end of the tennis match.

3.   During our picnic, John did not help with the cooking.

4.   Save the water in this cup for me.

B. Compound Subject and Compound Verb:

Directions: Cross out any prepositional phrase(s). Underline the
subject once and the verb or verb phrase twice.

**Remember: The subject or verb will not be a word in a prepositional
phrase.**

1.   Paper and pencils are on a table by the speaker.

2.   A child leaned over the railing and tossed a coin into the water.

C.   Can/May:

Directions: Circle the correct word.

1.   (Can, May) I go to the bathroom?

2.   I (can, may) understand your problem.   165

D. Contractions:

Directions: Write the contraction in the space provided.

1. were not - _____

2. where is - _____

3. we are - _____

4. should not - _____

5. you will - _____

6. did not - _____

7. you are - _____

8. I will - _____

9. cannot - _____

10. will not - _____

11. they are - _____

12. that is - _____

13. I have - _____

14. does not - _____

E. Direct Objects:

Directions: Underline the subject once and the verb twice. Label the direct object - D.O.

1. That dentist gives toothbrushes.

2. Our dog buried a bone.

3. We wash our car every Saturday.

F. Action?:

Directions: Write <u>Yes</u> if the boldfaced verb shows action. Write <u>No</u> if the boldfaced verb does not show action.

1. _____   The boy **looked** everywhere for his glasses.

2. _____   You **look** very pleased with yourself.

G. Regular or Irregular:

Directions: Write <u>RV</u> in the blank if the verb is regular. Write <u>IV</u> if the verb is irregular.

1. _____ to shake   2. _____ to bring   3. _____ to need

H. Helping (Auxiliary) Verbs:

Directions: Write the twenty-three helping verbs.

_____

_____

I. Subject/Verb Agreement:

Directions: Circle the correct verb.

1. My cat (meow, meows) softly.

2. Those birds (drink, drinks) from our birdbath.

3. I (stay, stays) inside after dinner.

J.   Irregular Verbs:

Directions: Cross out any prepositional phrase(s). Underline the
subject once and the verb or verb phrase twice.

1.   The football game has (began, begun).

2.   The canoe must have (sunk, sank).

3.   Allie should have (saw, seen) the comet!

4.   Have you (worn, wore) your new shoes?

5.   I could have (took, taken) the bus.

6.   Dad has not (got, gotten) the mail.

7.   Mrs. Hand should have (ran, run) for governor.

8.   The taxi cab has finally (came, come).

K.   Tenses:

Directions: Write the tense of the boldfaced verb.

Remember: The tenses are *present*, *past*, and *future*.

1.   _____   His mom **lifts** weights.

2.   _____   We **found** someone's wallet.

3.   _____   Franny **will fly** to Tulsa tomorrow.

A. Common and Proper Nouns:

Directions: Write a proper noun for each common noun.

1. town -_____

3. country -_____

2. actor -_____

4. ocean - _____

B. Common or Proper Nouns:

Directions: Write C if the noun is common. Write P if the noun is proper.

1. _____ COMB

3. _____ BUBBLE GUM

5. _____ HOUND

2. _____ RED SEA

4. _____ COMPUTER

6. _____ SUSAN

C. Singular and Plural Nouns:

Directions: Write the plural.

1. bush - _____

6. flame - _____

2. crutch - _____

7. mix - _____

3. pain - _____

8. goose - _____

4. elf - _____

9. day - _____

5. deer - _____

10. rodeo - _____

169

D. Possessive Nouns:

Directions: Write the possessive.

1.   shoes belonging to David - _____

2.   a locker shared by two girls - _____

3.   a store owned by more than one man - _____

4.   goldfish owned by Wendy -_____

E.   Noun Identification:

Directions: Circle any nouns.

🐢 **Remember:**   **A noun names a person, place, or thing.**
Look for "things" you can see.

1.   A groundhog ran across the road.

2.   Bess bought a puppy for her brother.

3.   A car and boat are parked by their house.

4.   His family goes to Kansas in a jet.

5.   Grandma keeps her watch in a tiny dish by her bed.

F. Adjectives (Describing Words):

Directions: Write two describing words for each noun.

1. _____   _____ bedspread

2. _____   _____ wagon

3. _____   _____ dress

G. A, An, and The:

Directions: Write *a* or *an* before each word or group of words.

1. _____ army   4. _____ octopus

2. _____ coat   5. _____ inch

3. _____ elm tree   6. _____ chocolate shake

H. Limiting Adjectives:

Directions: Fill in the blank.

1. _____, _____, and _____ are articles that are adjectives.

2. Write an example of a number used as an adjective: _____ horses.

3. Unscramble these adjectives that tell how many:

   a. laresve - _____   c. yanm - _____

   b. moes - _____   d. wfe -_____   171

Name_____   **Cumulative Review**
                                        Pronouns
Date_____

I.   Identifying Adjectives:

Directions: Circle each adjective.

🐢 **Remember:**   ***A**, **an**,* and ***the*** are adjectives.

Numbers and words like ***some**, **several**, **few**,*
many**, **no**,* and ***any can be limiting adjectives.

Most adjectives are describing words.

1.   A puffer fish swam in the blue water.

2.   Two large sheep grazed in an open field.

3.   I like banana splits with chopped nuts.

4.   Have any yellow birds flown by?

J.   Degrees of Adjectives:

Directions: Circle the correct form.

1.   Elaine is (taller, tallest) than her mother.

2.   He is the (heavier, heaviest) triplet.

3.   Your funny story is (interestinger, more interesting) than my scary one.

4.   This puppy is (more loveable, most loveable) of the litter.

5.   Of the two radios, the blue one has (better, best) sound.

172

A. Conjunctions:

Directions: Write <u>conj.</u> above each conjunction.

1.   Meg or her friend will take you to the airport.

2.   You may go, but take your brother and sister.

B. Interjections:

Directions: Write <u>intj.</u> above each interjection.

1.   Wow! You are very strong!

2.   I can do it!   Yeah!

C. Sentence Types:

Directions: Write the sentence type.

Remember: A **declarative** sentence makes a *statement.*
An **interrogative** sentence asks a *question.*
An **imperative** sentence gives a *command.*
An **exclamatory** **sentence** *shows emotion.*

1. _____ Who left?

2. _____ He left.

3. _____ Please leave.

4. _____ Yippee! We're leaving!

D.   **Adverbs That Tell How**:

Directions: Fill in the blank.

1.   Angie is a soft talker.

She talks _____.

2.   His face had a wide smile.

He smiled _____.

E.   **Adverbs That Tell How**:

Directions: Circle the adverb that tells *how*.

1.   The host laughed loudly.

2.   Corbin works harder in the evening.

3.   The little girl looked sadly at her father.

F.   **Adverbs That Tell When**:

Directions: Circle the adverb that tells *when*.

1. We must do it now.

2. Tonight, I hope to see a shooting star.

3. Mrs. Robb visits her mother daily.

4.   I never put sugar on my cereal.
174

G.   Adverbs That Tell Where:

   Directions: Circle the adverb that tells *where*.

1. Stay there.

2. Where are you going?

3. Please come inside.

H.   Adverbs That Tell to What Extent:

   Directions: Circle the adverb that tells *to what extent*.

1. He answered very rudely.

2. This ball has become rather flat.

3. You swim quite well.

I.   Degrees of Adverbs:

   Directions: Circle the correct form.

1. She hit the ball (harder, hardest) during her second time at bat.

2. I write (more sloppily, most sloppily) with my left hand.

3. Rob draws animals (better, weller) than people.

4. The banker spoke (more kindly, most kindly) to his third client.

5. Michael skates (more rapidly, most rapidly) than his older brother.   175

Name_____   **CAPITALIZATION**

Date_____

Rule 1: **Capitalize a person's name.**

Examples: Leela

Jonah Boyd

Rule 2: **Capitalize initials.**

Examples: Pippa **A.** Begay

T. C. Bota

Rule 3: **Capitalize a title with a name.**

Examples: Uncle Carlos   **Miss C.** Como

Grandma **W**ong   Doctor Cohen

Rule 4: **Capitalize the pronoun _I_.**

Rule 5: **Capitalize the first word of a sentence.**

🐢 🐢 🐢 🐢 🐢 🐢 🐢 🐢 🐢 🐢 🐢 🐢 🐢 🐢 🐢 🐢 🐢 🐢

Directions: Write your answer on the line.

1. Write your first, middle, and last name. _____

2. Write your first name with your middle initial. _____

3. Write your three initials. _____

4. Write your aunt's name or uncle's name with the title. _____

5. Answer this question in a complete sentence: _What is your favorite_

food? _____

6. Write a complete sentence using the pronoun _I_.

_____

Date_____

Rule 6:   **Capitalize days of the week.**
            Examples: **S**unday   **T**hursday

Rule 7:   **Capitalize months of the year.**
            Examples: **M**arch   **S**eptember

Rule 8:   **Capitalize holidays.**
            Examples: **M**emorial **D**ay   **P**residents' **D**ay

Rule 9:   **Capitalize special days.**
            Examples: **F**ather's **D**ay   **V**alentine's **D**ay

🐢 🐢 🐢 🐢 🐢 🐢 🐢 🐢 🐢 🐢 🐢 🐢 🐢 🐢 🐢 🐢 🐢 🐢 🐢
Directions: Write your answer on the line.

1.   Write the days of the week. _____, _____,

_____, _____, _____,

_____, and _____.

2.   Write the name of your favorite month. _____

3.   Write the name of your favorite holiday. _____

4.   Write the name of the special day on this list that you like best:
     St. **P**atrick's **D**ay   **V**alentine's **D**ay
     Ground **H**og's **D**ay.   **A**rbor **D**ay

_____

5.   My favorite day is _____ because _____

_____

Rule 10:   **Capitalize the names of streets, roads, avenues, drives, lanes, highways, trails, turnpikes, and other roadways.**

Examples: Redwood Street   Lincoln Highway
Bull Road   Pioneer Trail
Cooper Avenue   Everett Turnpike
Castle Drive   Swope Parkway
Park Lane   Range Boulevard

Capitalize <u>directions</u> when they appear with a name of a roadway.
South State Street

Rule 11:   **Capitalize the name of a town or city.**
Examples: Bendersville   Jackson

Rule 12:   **Capitalize the name of a state.**
Examples: Maryland   Idaho

Rule 13:   **Capitalize the name of a country.**
Examples: China   France

🐢 🐢 🐢 🐢 🐢 🐢 🐢 🐢 🐢 🐢 🐢 🐢 🐢 🐢 🐢 🐢 🐢 🐢

Directions: Write your answer on the line.

1.   Write the name of your country. _____

2.   Write the name of your state. _____

3.   Write the name of your town or city. _____

4.   Write the name of a street or other roadway. _____

5.   Write the name of a state you would like to visit. _____

178

Name_____ **CAPITALIZATION**

Date_____

Directions: Write the capital letter above any word that needs to be capitalized.

1.   does randy live on coco avenue?

2.   in august, I went to alabama.

3.   did uncle harry buy a new car?

4.   i gave cindy candy on valentine's day.

5.   his cousin lives in macon, georgia.

6.   brian and i went to the library on penn street.

7.   becky a. smith moved to elk city.

8.   her aunt is coming on the third tuesday in april.

9.   on memorial day, his family went to mexico.

10.   did dr. hamel move his office to east dell street?

11.   last saturday, mr. sites visited ash, north carolina.

12.   during christmas vacation, he always goes to canada.

13.   we will visit grandma metz on wednesday or thursday.

14.   Our new address is 20 linx lane, akron, ohio 44333.

15.   are sandy and i invited to your st. patrick's day party?

Date_____

Rule 14: **Capitalize the name of a school or college.**

Examples: Sky View School   Ball College

Rule 15: **Capitalize the name of a library or hospital.**

Examples: Adams County Library
Fountain Valley Hospital

Rule 16: **Capitalize the name of a store, a restaurant, or another business.**

Examples: Tang's Grocery
Mon Ton Department Store
Sesame Restaurant
Gotta Go Travel Agency
Reno Construction Company
Music Box Theater

If *in*, *to*, *for*, *of*, or other prepositions of four or less letters appear as part of the name, do <u>not</u> capitalize them. Also, do <u>not</u> capitalize *a*, *an*, *the*, *and*, *but*, *nor*, and *or* unless they are the first or last word.
Jack and Jill Shop
Food with a Flair Restaurant

🐢 🐢 🐢 🐢 🐢 🐢 🐢 🐢 🐢 🐢 🐢 🐢 🐢 🐢 🐢 🐢 🐢 🐢

Directions: Write your answer on the line.

1. Write the name of your favorite school. _____

2. Write the name of a college. _____

3. Write the name of a library in your town. _____

4. Write the name of a hospital in your area. _____

5. Write the name of a store in your area. _____

Date_____

Rule 17: **Capitalize the name of a language.**

Examples: **E**nglish **S**panish

Rule 18: **Capitalize the first word of a direct quotation.** (A direct quotation is when someone says something.)

Example: Richard asked, "**W**here are my jeans?"

Rule 19: **Capitalize the first word in a line of poetry.**
These are lines from a poem entitled "At Home" by Christina Rossetti.
Examples: **M**ix a pancake,
Stir a pancake,

Rule 20: **Capitalize the first word of a greeting in a letter.**

Example: **D**ear Zak,

Rule 21: **Capitalize the first word of a closing in a letter.**

Example: **S**incerely yours,

🐢 🐢 🐢 🐢 🐢 🐢 🐢 🐢 🐢 🐢 🐢 🐢 🐢 🐢 🐢 🐢 🐢 🐢

Directions: Write your answer on the line.

1. The language I speak is _____.

2. Write something you have said: I said, " _____."

3. Write the second line of this poem:

   Jack and Jill went up the hill,

   _____

4. Write a greeting of a letter beginning with *dear*. _____

5. Write the closing of a letter beginning with *your*. _____

Date_____

Directions: Write the capital letter above any word that needs to be capitalized.

1.   we ate breakfast at golden nugget cafe.

2.   my brother attends arizona state university.

3.   the lady checked out a spanish book from mesa public library.

4.   my dear friend,

        here are the pictures of our vacation.

                your friend,
                amy

5.   these are my favorite lines from a poem:
        you dance to the music of a lonely fife,
        and I march to the beat of a distant drum.

6.   she said, "let's listen to the radio."

7.   has spar high school opened yet?

8.   grandma entered york hospital for tests.

9.   they work at winston general store.

10.   is your neighbor studying french at scottsdale junior college?

11.   her dad works for blair insurance agency.

12.   our family went out to eat at silver swan restaurant.

Rule 22: **Capitalize Roman numerals, the major divisions and the first word in an outline.**

> Example: **I. M**ammals
> **A. W**hales
> **B. D**olphins and porpoises

Rule 23: **Capitalize the first word, the last word, and all important words in titles. Do *not* capitalize *a, an, the, and, but, or, nor,* or prepositions of four or less letters unless they are the first or the last word.**

> Examples: <u>**P**rayer</u>
> "**S**ilent **N**ight"
> <u>**B**irth of **L**iberty</u>
> <u>**E**ight **L**ittle **P**igs</u>
> "**A T**ruck for **W**illie"
> <u>**T**he **C**at **W**ho **W**ent to **P**aris</u>

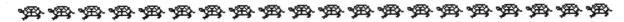

A. Directions: Capitalize this outline.

   i. history

      a. american history

      b. world history

B. Directions: Capitalize these titles.

   1. "thirteen"

   2. <u>my country</u>

   3. <u>deer of the world</u>

   4. <u>the iron horse</u>   183

Rule 24:   Capitalize the name of a particular building.

_____Examples: church, temple, or synagogue - **Temple Beth Emeth**
tower - **Little Roundtop Tower**
house - **Dobbin House**
museum - **Thomas Edison Museum**
lighthouse - **Bodie Island Lighthouse**
airport - **Deer Valley Airport**

Rule 25:   Capitalize the name of a particular place.

stream - **Potato Creek**   island - **Cedar Island**

lake - **Liberty Lake**   desert - **Sonoran Desert**

river - **Wabash River**   forest - **Turtle Mt. State Forest**

sea - **Salton Sea**   park - **Yellowstone National Park**

ocean - **Atlantic Ocean**   hill(s) - **Fox Hill**

beach - **Bonita Beach**   mountain(s) - **Ozark Mountains**

🐢🐢🐢🐢🐢🐢🐢🐢🐢🐢🐢🐢🐢🐢🐢🐢🐢🐢🐢

Directions: Write the capital letter above any word that needs to be capitalized.

1.   have you been to flathead lake?

2.   does the heard museum have paintings?

3.   we have visited reedy island.

4.   Their family attends sacred heart church.

5.   they went to bear mountain state park yesterday.

6.   is rye beach on the atlantic ocean?

Name_____ **DO NOT CAPITALIZE**

Date_____

Rule 1:   **Do not capitalize seasons of the year.**
        spring   summer   winter   fall (autumn)

Rule 2:   **Do not capitalize directions.**
        north   south   east   west

   However, capitalize these when they appear as part of a place name.
        Patty lives at 882 **North** Ocean View Drive.

Rule 3:   **Do not capitalize foods, games, plants, or animals.**
            food - apple pie
            game - tag
            plant - daisy
            animal - muskrat

   However, if a country's name appears with it, capitalize the country but not the food, game, plant, or animal.
            food - **M**exican rice   (Mexico)
            game - **C**hinese checkers   (China)
            plant - **B**ermuda grass   (Bermuda)
            animal - **G**erman shepherd   (Germany)

🐢 🐢 🐢 🐢 🐢 🐢 🐢 🐢 🐢 🐢 🐢 🐢 🐢 🐢 🐢 🐢 🐢 🐢 🐢
Directions: Write your answer on the line.

1.   A game I like is _____.

2.   The direction I live from the closest town is _____.

3.   My favorite season of the year is _____.

4.   My favorite food is _____.

5.   My favorite animal is a _____.   185

Date_____

Directions: Write the capital letter above any word that needs to be capitalized.

1. let's go to the catskill mountains in july.

2. the country of mexico is south of arizona.

3. sheldon museum was built in 1829.

4. dear paula,

    yesterday, we went to garfield park in chicago.

    your friend,

    mandy

5. the gotland islands are in the baltic sea.

6. dave asked, "why don't you learn french?"

7. on thanksgiving, i attended hope baptist church.

8. Capitalize these titles:

    a. "trouble"

    b. eva's story

    c. butterflies and moths

    d. read with me

Name_____   **CAPITALIZATION**
                                     Review
Date_____

Directions: Write the capital letter above any word that needs to be
               capitalized.

1.   karen takes classes at wheaton college.

2.   last friday, they fished at mirror lake.

3.   does your mom shop at marsh country store?

4.   she likes these two lines from a poem by gene fowler:

          i carry boulders across the day

          from the field to the ridge.

5.   is sugar loaf mountain in new hampshire?

6.   someone gave a tulip tree to chambersburg hospital.

7.   Capitalize this outline:

          i.   movies

               a.   comedies

               b.   scary movies

8.   in august, uncle ralph will visit iowa.

9.   does little lost river flow into the pacific ocean?

10.   next tuesday, doctor roy p. lamb will speak to us.

Directions: Write the capital letter above any word that needs to be capitalized.

1.   the mohawk trail is in new york.

2.   my brother read <u>flying the mail</u>.

3.   he and i leave national airport on sunday.

4.   last winter, mark camped by miller creek.

5.   amba attends sunrise elementary school.

6.   juan asked, "are you taking your dog?"

7.   we celebrate veterans' day in november.

8.   my dear cousin,

        we are going to crater national park tomorrow!

                love,

                lani

9.   have you been to the henry ford museum?

10.   we ate at food king after checking out books at peoria library.

11.   on thursday, july 16, the couple married at holy trinity greek cathedral.

12.   his address is 22 ridge street, gettysburg, pennsylvania   17325.

PUNCTUATION
Period (.)

Rule 1: **Place a period at the end of a declarative sentence.**
(A declarative sentence makes a *statement*.)

Example: Her arm is broken.

Rule 2: **Place a period at the end of an imperative sentence.**
(An imperative sentence gives a *command*.)

Example: Pick that up.

Rule 3: **Place a period after initials.**

Example: Hope R. Lang

Rule 4: **Place a period after an abbreviation for a day of the week.**

Sunday - Sun.	Tuesday - Tues., Tue.*	Thursday - Thurs., Thur.*
Monday - Mon.	Wednesday - Wed.	Friday - Fri.
*The first is preferred.		Saturday - Sat.

Directions: Write your answer on the line.

1. My friend's initials are _____.

2. Write a declarative sentence:

    _____

3. Write an imperative sentence: _____

4. Unscramble these days of the week and then write the abbreviation:

    a. ytradhsu - _____ _____   c. dtausey - _____ _____

    b. tadasryu - _____ _____   d. yfaird - _____ _____

189

Rule 5:   **Place a period after the abbreviation for each month.**

January - Jan.	April - Apr.	October - Oct.
February - Feb.	August - Aug.	November - Nov.
March - Mar.	September - Sept.	December - Dec.

May, June, and July do not have abbreviations.

Rule 6:   **Place a period after the abbreviation for titles.**

Mr. - Mister
Mrs. - title used for a married woman's name
Ms. - title that does not show if a woman is married or unmarried
Dr. - Doctor

Do not place a period after *Miss* used as a title: Miss Brown

Rule 7:   **Place a period after the abbreviation for some places.**

St. - Street	Middle St.
Ave. - Avenue	91st Ave.
Ln. - Lane	Laurel Ln.
Dr. - Drive	Dunn Dr.
Rd. - Road	Tanner Road
Mt. - Mountain	Turtle Mt.
Mts. - Mountains	Pioneer Mts.

U. S. - United States or U. S. A. - United States of America

Always use a dictionary to check for correct abbreviations.

Use the two letter postal code **without a period** for state abbreviations.

NY - New York   NE - Nebraska

Directions: Write the abbreviation.

1.   The month I begin school is _____. Christmas is in

_____. The month which I like best is _____.

2.   a.   Judd Lane - _____   c.   Mister Ling - _____

b.   United States - _____   d.   Elk Mountain - _____

Rule 1: **Use an apostrophe in a contraction to show where a letter or letters have been left out.**

cannot - can't   he is - he's

Rule 2: **Use an apostrophe to show ownership.**

A. **If one item owns something, add ' + s̲.**

Examples: Brad**'s** room   pen**'s** cap

B. **If a word is plural (more than one) and ends in s̲, add ' after the s̲ to show ownership.**

Example: dog**s'** dish   (the dish belongs to more than one dog)

C. **If a word is plural (more than one) and does not end in s, add ' + s̲ to show ownership.**

Examples: children**'s** room   men**'s** shirts

Directions: Write the answer in the blank.

1.   Write your first name: _____.   Name something that you

own: _____.   Now, use *rule 2A* to write your name and

the item that you own: _____.

2.   a.   a pet belonging to a boy - _____

b.   a pet belonging to two boys - _____

c.   toys belonging to one child - _____

d.   toys shared by many children - _____

A.   Directions: Write the abbreviation for each day of the week.

1.   Wednesday - _____   5.   Thursday - _____

2.   Saturday - _____   6.   Monday - _____

3.   Tuesday - _____   7.   Friday - _____

4.   Sunday - _____

B.   Directions: Write the abbreviation for the month of the year.

1.   January - _____   6.   September - _____

2.   February - _____   7.   October - _____

3.   March - _____   8.   November - _____

4.   April - _____   9.   December - _____

5.   August - _____

C.   Directions: Place a period or an apostrophe where needed.

1.   I cant go with Mrs Kline

2.   Mikes brother lives on Fawn St

3.   The White Mts arent very high

4.   Mail this U S map for me

5.   Dr Harton talked about his three nurses vacations

192

PUNCTUATION
Comma (,)

Rule 1:   **Place a comma between the day and year in a date.**
            Example: April 1, 1999

Rule 2:   **Place a comma between the name of a day and date.**
            Example: Monday, July 21, 1997

Rule 3:   **Place a comma between a town or city and a state.**
            Examples: Altus, Oklahoma
                       Nashville, Tennessee

Rule 4:   **Place a comma between a city and a country.**
            Example: Mexico City, Mexico

Rule 5:   **In a street address, place a comma after the street and after the city.**
            Do not place a comma between a state and the zip code.
            Do not place a comma between the house number and a street name.

            Example: I live at 12 North Easy Street, Carefree, AZ   85529.
                                     ↑ (no comma)   ↑ (no comma)

Directions: Read each sentence and complete it.

1.   Write today's date: _____.

2.   Write the day of the week and today's date: _____.

3.   Write your town (city) and your state: _____.

4.   Write your street address: _____.

5.   Place commas in this address: 2 Arc Lane Clinton SC* 29325.
            *the state of South Carolina   193

Rule 6:   **Place a comma after three or more items in a series.**
Do not place a comma after the last item in a series.

    Example: I bought pretzels, chips, and soda for our party.

                                                                ⬆ (no comma)

Do not place a comma between two items.
    Example: celery and carrots

Rule 7:   **Place a comma after the greeting of a friendly letter.**
    Example: Dear Randy,

Rule 8:   **Place a comma after the closing of a friendly letter.**
    Example: Your friend,

Rule 9:   **Place a comma after a word like *yes* or *no* at the beginning of a sentence.**

    Example: No, I don't want any dessert.

🐢 🐢 🐢 🐢 🐢 🐢 🐢 🐢 🐢 🐢 🐢 🐢 🐢 🐢 🐢 🐢 🐢 🐢

Directions: Read each sentence and complete it.

1.   Write a greeting of a letter to one of your friends: _____.

2.   Write a closing of a letter to someone: _____.

3.   Finish this sentence: My three best friends are _____

_____.

4.   Place commas where needed:

    a.   Yes I would like some chips and dip.

    b.   Gary Annette and Sammy won!

194

Rule 10: **Place a comma when speaking to someone.**

a. **If the name of the person is at the beginning of a sentence, place a comma after the person's name.**

Example: Hansel, when is your birthday?

b. **If the name of the person is at the end of a sentence, place a comma before the person's name.**

Example: I like your sweater, Jana.

Rule 11: **Place a comma in a direct quotation.**
A direct quotation states exactly what the person says.

Example: "I'm too tired to race again," said Dena.

If the person who is talking is given first, place a comma after the person's name + *said* or *asked*.

Example: Yancy asked, "Why are you leaving?"

Directions: Place commas where needed.

1. Lani said "Let's buy some candy."

2. Seth will you hand me that hammer?

3. "Thanks for your help " said Kammie.

4. I'll be right back Howi.

5. Mrs. Reno asked "Where is Rose Lane?"

Name_____   **PUNCTUATION**
Using Commas

Date_____

Directions: Place commas where needed.

1.   Dear Joan

   I'll see your next week in Florida.

        Forever friends

        Stacey

2.   The couple was married on June 28 1996.

3.   Yes we want you to come with us.

4.   "A diamond is harder than an opal " said the teacher.

5.   Billy this lumber is too soft.

6.   He is taking a towel lotion and a radio to the beach.

7.   Their aunt and uncle live in Austin Texas.

8.   She was born on Thursday May 20 1982.

9.   Dottie's address is 59 Hutton Avenue Toney AL 35773.

10.   Gwen asked "How is your father?"

11.   Please mail this card Jackie.

12.   No they aren't serving ice cream and cake.

13.   Fred Nan and Terry are flying to Paris France.

Name_____

Date_____

Colon (:):

Rule: **Place a colon between the hour and minute(s) in time.**

Example: It's 2:15 P. M.

Question Mark (?):

Rule: **Place a question mark at the end of a sentence that asks a question.**

Example: Do you have any money**?**

Exclamation Point (Mark) (!):

Rule 1: **Place an exclamation point after an interjection.**

Remember: An interjection shows emotion.
An interjection is not a complete sentence.

Example: Wow!

Rule 2: **Place an exclamation point after a sentence that shows emotion.**

Example: We've finally landed!

🐢 🐢 🐢 🐢 🐢 🐢 🐢 🐢 🐢 🐢 🐢 🐢 🐢 🐢 🐢 🐢 🐢 🐢

Directions: Place a colon, question mark, or exclamation point where needed.

1. The meeting will start at 8 00 P. M.

2. Yeah We're the champs

3. Bob exclaimed, "I'm allowed to go "

4. Does the picnic begin at 4 30 in the afternoon

Name_____

Date_____

Underlining (_):

> **Rule 1:**   **Underline the title of a book.**
> Example: The child's mom reads <u>Corduroy</u> to him.

> **Rule 2:**   **Underline the title of a magazine.**
> Example: I like <u>Bees and Bugs</u>.

> **Rule 3:**   **Underline the title of a newspaper.**
> Example: My uncle always reads <u>Current Times</u>.

> **Rule 4:**   **Underline the title of a movie or television show.**
> Example: Dad likes to watch <u>Travels with Ama</u>.

Directions: Complete each sentence.

1.   My favorite book when I was little was _____.

2.   My favorite book now is _____.

3.   My favorite movie is _____.

4.   My favorite television show is _____.

5.   The name of a magazine is _____.

6.   The name of a newspaper is _____.

198

Quotation Marks (" "):

Rule 1: **Place quotation marks around a direct quotation.**
A direct quotation is what someone says.
> Example: Matt said, "Let's play basketball."

Rule 2: **Place quotation marks around the title of a short story.**
> Example: Dad read the story, "Angus and the Cat," to us.

Rule 3: **Place quotation marks around the title of a poem.**
> Example: She likes the poem, "White Season."

Rule 4: **Place quotation marks around the title of a song.**
> Example: "Don't Tell My Heart" was a popular song.

Rule 5: **Place quotation marks around the title of a chapter.**
> Example: The first chapter of our science book is "Plants."

Directions: Complete each sentence.

1. My favorite song is _____.

2. The name of a short story is _____.

3. The name of a poem is _____.

4. The name of a chapter in a book is _____.

5. Write something you have said: _____

_____said _____ (your name).   199

Name_____

Date_____

Directions: Use quotation marks or underlining where needed.

1. Kali said,   That's my coat.

2. We watched the movie, Abel's Island.

3. They sang The Mitten Song after lunch.

4. Casper read the book named Elmo the Pig.

5. We read the short story, Sylvester and the Magic Pebble.

6. He watched Cooking with Kana on television.

7. We opened our science book to the chapter, Bugs.

8. Mother often reads the magazine, Patterns.

9. My favorite poem is Snowball Wind.

10. Will you carry this for me?   asked Chika.

11. The title of my mother's favorite short story is The Necklace.

12. Dad read the book, The Songwriters Idea Book.

13. The lady at the airport read the newspaper, Spotlight News.

A. Periods:

Directions: Place periods where needed.

1.   Mr Dine lives on Rabbit Rd

2.   Write the abbreviation for each day of the week:

a.   Sunday - _____   c.   Tuesday - _____   e.   Thursday - _____

b.   Monday - _____   d.   Wednesday - _____   f.   Friday - _____

g.   Saturday - _____

3.   Write the abbreviation for these months:

a.   January - _____   d.   September - _____

b.   February - _____   e.   October - _____

c.   August - _____   f.   December - _____

B. Apostrophes:

Directions: Place apostrophes where needed.

1.   She hasnt washed her truck.

2.   Brians dog is a German shepherd.

3.   The boys bathroom is down the hall.

4.   His mens baseball team plays tonight.

Date_____

C. Commas:

Directions: Place commas where needed.

1. Millie lives in Chicago Illinois.

2. Yes I'll be there.

3. She likes eggs ham and toast for breakfast.

4. Ted I want to talk to you.

5. "I'd like two slices of pizza " said Leslie.

6. They met on January 1 1995.

7. Will you loan me your skates Pam?

8. His parents went to London England.

9. Dear Julie

   May I stay with you this weekend?

   Love

   Denise

10. Her next appointment is Friday August 11 2000.

11. Their new address is 12 Bridge Street Elkton Maryland 21922.

PUNCTUATION
Review

D. Colons, Question Marks, and Exclamation Points:

Directions: Place colons, question marks, or exclamation points where needed.

1. Does your grandfather plant a garden

2. Yippee   It's recess

3. They arrived at 11 15 A. M.

E.   Underlining and Quotation Marks:

Directions: Underline or use quotation marks where needed.

1. Titles:

a. book: The Beatle Bush

b. short story: Here, Puppy

c. movie: Baby's Bedtime

d. poem: At the Zoo

e. song: Here's a Happy Song

f. newspaper: Frogtown News

g. magazine: Beaches

2. Brody said,   It's nice to meet you.

Writing Formal Notes:

To write a formal note:

1. If desired, place the date in the upper right hand corner (about one-half to one inch from the top) with the last digit of the year ending with your right margin.

2. Skip down a line or two on the note paper to write your greeting.
    a. The number of lines you skip depends on the length of the message, your handwriting size, and the size of the paper.

    b. The message should not be "bunched" at the top of the note but flow down the page.

3. The greeting should begin at your left margin. (Be sure to place a comma after the greeting.)

4. The message (or body) should be indented. Indent five spaces.

5. Write your closing. (Be sure to place a comma after it.)

6. Write your name directly under the first letter of your closing.

July 23, 1997	**date**
Dear Grandma,	**greeting**
Thanks for my birthday card and money. I want to use the money for a new jacket.	**message (body)**
How are you? Are you still coming to visit us at Christmas? I hope so.	
Love,	**closing**
Ginger	**signature**

FRIENDLY LETTER

The parts of a friendly letter are the **heading**, the **greeting**, the **body (message)**, the **closing**, and the **signature**.

A three-lined **formal** heading will be used. In **informal** letters, the date is frequently the only item included. However, the formal heading is important to know.

In a formal letter, as in all formal writing, abbreviations are not used.

The **exception** to this is the postal code for states. A postal code is capitalized, and no punctuation is used.

Examples: South Dakota = SD   Oklahoma = OK
Wyoming = WY   Michigan = MI

🐢 🐢 🐢 🐢 🐢 🐢 🐢 🐢 🐢 🐢 🐢 🐢 🐢 🐢 🐢 🐢 🐢 🐢 🐢

Friendly Letter Parts:

                              HOUSE NUMBER AND STREET NAME
heading   CITY, STATE   ZIP CODE
                              COMPLETE DATE (not abbreviated)

greeting Dear (Person)   ,

                  The body is also called the message. It is written here.

            Indent at least five spaces. You may skip a line between the

body   greeting and the body. Note that you have margins on each

            side of the paper.

         closing   Truly yours,

         signature   Your Name   205

MY OWN NOTES

A sentence expresses a complete thought. The subject of a sentence is **who** or **what** the sentence is about.

> **Example:** A little girl danced.

We are talking about a girl. *Girl* is the subject of the sentence.

ॐॐॐ

Sometimes, the sentence is about more than one thing.

> **Example:** A little girl and her sister danced.

We are talking about the girl **and** her sister. *Girl* and *sister* are the

subject of the sentence. We call this a **compound subject**.

Usually, we use **and** to join two words in a compound subject.

ॐॐॐॐॐॐॐॐॐॐॐॐ

Directions: Use **and** to join the subject of two sentences.

> **Example:** Pedro painted a chair. Tony painted, too.
>
> **Pedro and Tony painted a chair.**

1. Mom played in a softball game. Dad played in a softball game.

   _____

   _____

2. Eggs were served for breakfast. Muffins were served for breakfast, too.

   _____

   _____

3. The boys ride bikes to school. The girls ride bikes to school.

_____

_____

4. Our grandmother baked cookies. Our grandfather baked cookies.

_____

_____

5. Jan wanted to sail. Her brother wanted to sail, also.

_____

_____

6. Ice will melt quickly in hot weather. Ice cream will melt quickly
   in hot weather.

_____

_____

7. Lani washed cherries for a fruit salad. Moe washed cherries, too.

_____

_____

8. Tulips are blooming. Daisies are blooming.

_____

_____

MY OWN NOTES

Name_____ **Writing Sentences**

Date_____ **Items in a Series**

A sentence expresses a complete thought. The subject of a sentence is **who** or **what** the sentence is about.

Example: Candy or Eric will cut the melons.

We are talking about Candy or Eric. <u>Candy</u> + <u>Eric</u> = **compound subject**. Sometimes, we use **or** to join two words in a compound subject.

෴෴෴෴෴෴෴෴෴෴෴

Directions: Use **or** to join the subject of two sentences.

Example: Pat made peanut butter sandwiches.
Kim may have made peanut butter sandwiches.

Pat or Kim made peanut butter sandwiches.

1. Jana won the game. Devi may have won the game.

_____

_____

2. A neighbor built the fence. Her friend may have built the fence.

_____

_____

3. Hamburgers may be served for dinner. Tacos may be served instead.

_____

_____

4. My sister will march in a parade. My brother may take her place.

_____

_____

MY OWN NOTES

The subject of a sentence is **who** or **what** the sentence is about. **Sometimes, a verb may change.**

> **Example:** Min wants a snack. Suzy wants a snack, too.

When we talk about one (singular), we use a singular verb. Each person **wants** a snack. However, when we join *Min and Suzy*, we make a compound subject. The verb must agree with the plural (more than one) subject. Therefore, Min and Suzy **want** a snack.

ॐॐॐ

A verb may change form with a compound subject.

> **Example:** My foot is swollen. My ankle is also swollen.

When we talk about one (singular), we use a singular verb. When we are talking about two or more joined by **and**, we must use a verb that agrees.

> Wrong: My foot and ankle **is** swollen.

> Right: My foot and ankle **are** swollen.

ॐॐॐॐॐॐॐॐॐॐॐ

Directions: Use **and** to join the subjects of two sentences.

Example: Tyger likes car races. Chris likes car races, too.

Tyger and Chris like car races.

1. Luis eats lunch late. Annie eats lunch late, too.

_____

_____

2. Kirk is a model.   Lisa is a model, also.

_____

_____

3. Her mother sews costumes for our school plays. His aunt sews costumes for our school plays.

_____

_____

4. Their sister wants to go to a beach this summer. Their brother wants to go to a beach this summer.

_____

_____

5. Misty goes to soccer practice on Mondays. Marc goes to soccer practice on Mondays, too.

_____

_____

6. Mr. Liss was a pilot. His wife was a pilot, also.

_____

_____

7. Dad is standing by the door. My uncle is standing by the door, too.

_____

_____

MY OWN NOTES

Two items can be joined by **and**. <u>They do not have to join the subject</u> of a sentence.

     Examples: She *sang* and *whistled*.

                    Mom buys *juice* and *water*.

                    He and *I* are good friends.

                    Her hair is *short* and *curly*.

                    They looked *up* and *down*.

                    ∾∾∾

Sometimes, <u>three or more</u> items are joined.

    Example: Jason has keys, coins, and a comb in his pocket.

Place a comma after the items in a series that occur before *and*. Do no place a comma after ***and/or*** or after the *last item*.

    Example: Do you want water, a soda, juice, or milk to drink?

             ∾∾∾∾∾∾∾∾∾∾∾∾

Directions: Join sentences.

     Example: The farmer owns a cow.
                         The farmer owns five goats.
                         The farmer owns ten hens.

       <u>**The farmer owns a cow, five goats, and ten hens.**</u>

1. The chef made bread. The chef made a salad. The chef made a dessert.

    _____

    _____

2. Bob is going to a baseball game.
   Tara is going to a baseball game.
   Luis is going to a baseball game, too.

   _____

   _____

3. A girl stood.
   She waved.
   She cheered.

   _____

   _____

4. I want to hike with Kim.
   I want to hike with Josh.
   I want to hike with Emily, also.

   _____

   _____

5. Jana's grandma sends her cards.
   Jana's grandma sends her posters.
   Jana's grandma sends her pictures of tigers.

   _____

   _____

6. An elephant stopped.
   An elephant tilted his head from side to side.
   An elephant lifted his trunk, also.

   _____

   _____

Two or more items can be joined by a conjunction. A conjunction is
and, **or**, or **but**.

Examples: *Mike, Moe,* and *Mia* are triplets.   **(nouns-subject)**

The bug *flew* by, *buzzed*, and *landed*.   **(verbs)**

Give your books to *him* and *me*.   **(pronouns)**

Our teacher is *smart, funny,* and *strict*.   **(adjectives)**

The judge spoke *slowly, clearly, and kindly*.   **(adverbs)**

Place a comma when there are more than two items in a series.
Do not place a comma after *and/or/but* or after the *last item*.
✤✤✤
Sometimes, the verb will change.

Examples: Cheese **is** on the table.
Fruit **is** on the table.
Bread **is** on the table.

Cheese, fruit, and bread are on the table.

Kit **owns** a scooter.
Parker **owns** a scooter.
Lisa **owns** a scooter.

Kit, Parker, and Lisa own a scooter.
✤✤✤✤✤✤✤✤✤✤✤
Directions: Join sentences.

1.   Movies are sold at the video store.
Games are sold at the video store.
Comics are sold at the video store.

_____

_____

2. The man ordered fish.
   He ordered chips.
   He ordered lemonade.

   _____

   _____

3. Hannah has a goldfish.
   Her brother has a goldfish.
   Her sister has a goldfish, also.

   _____

   _____

4. The patient smiled.
   The patient opened his mouth.
   The patient stuck out his tongue.

   _____

   _____

5. Lana walks to her mailbox.
   Lana sometimes skips to her mailbox.
   Sometimes, Lana hops to her mailbox.

   _____

   _____

6. Tate walks with his mother to his baseball games.
   Tate sometimes walks with his dad to his baseball games.
   Tate sometimes walks with his sisters to his baseball games.

   _____

   _____

An appositive is a word or group of words that explains something in a sentence.

> **Example:**   We are looking for Banter.

Who is Banter? We don't know. Now look at the sentence with words that explain who Banter is. These words are called an **appositive**.

An appositive is placed <u>next to</u> the word it explains.

> **Example:**   We are looking for Banter, **his lost dog**.
>   **appositive**

An appositive is set off by commas.

> **Example:**   Miss Sue, **a teacher**, bikes to school.
>   ↕   ↕
>   We heard a noise, **a loud scream**.
>   ↕

ॐॐॐॐॐॐॐॐॐॐ

Directions: Place the appositive by the word it explains.

> **Example:**   They watched *Mary Poppins*.
>   *Mary Poppins* is their favorite musical.

<u>**They watched *Mary Poppins*, *their favorite musical.***</u>

1. Sandy is a dentist.
    Sandy is their cousin.

    Sandy, _____ **, is a dentist.**

2. Marty is a classmate.
   Marty won a writing contest.

   _____ **Marty,** _____ **, won a writing** _____

   _____ **contest.** _____

3. I nearly stepped on a slug.
   A slug is a slimy animal.

   _____ **I nearly stepped on a slug,** _____

   _____

4. Iceland is near the Arctic Circle.
   Iceland is an island.

   _____ **Iceland,** _____ **, is near the Arctic** _____

   _____ **Circle.** _____

5. Have you eaten a mango? Mango is a fruit grown in Hawaii.

   _____ **Have you eaten a mango,** _____

   _____

6. We saw mica at a rock show.
   Mica is a shiny mineral.

   _____ **We saw mica,** _____ **, at a rock** _____

   _____ **show.** _____

An appositive is a word or group of words that explains something in a sentence.

> **Example:**   Mike is coming to visit.

   Who is Mike? We don't know. Now look at the sentence with words that explain who Mike is. These words are called an **appositive**.

> **Example:**   Mike, **my uncle**, is coming to visit.
>   appositive

An appositive is placed <u>next to</u> the word it explains.

> **Example:**   I love Sassy, their cat.
>   appositive

An appositive is set off by commas.

> **Example:**   Miss Pinky, **our pony**, was a gift.
>   ↕   ↕
>   Cass is going to Harney, **her hometown.**
>   ↕

ֆ֎ֆ֎ֆ֎ֆ֎ֆ֎ֆ֎ֆ֎ֆ֎ֆ֎ֆ֎

Directions: Place the appositive by the word it explains.

> **Example:**   Gee is fun.
>   Gee is his grandmother.

> **Gee,** _____ **, is fun.**

> **Gee,** _his grandmother_**, is fun.**

1.   Jim left for college.
     Jim is my brother.

> **Jim,** _____ **, left for college.**

2. Kimmy ran after her pet.
    Her pet is a goose.

    _____ **Kimmy ran after her pet,** _____

3. That lady is pretty.
    That lady is my mother.

    _____ **That lady,** _____ **, is pretty.** _____

4. Layla gave me a present.
    It was a yoyo.

    _____ **Layla gave me a present,** _____

5. Mrs. Pope is a judge. Mrs. Pope took a vacation.

    _____ **Mrs. Pope,** _____ **, took a**

    _____ **vacation.** _____

6. He plays a fife.
    A fife is a musical instrument similar to a flute

    _____ **He plays a fife,** _____

    _____

7. The town built a new building.
    The building is a six-story hospital.

    _____ **The town built a new building,** _____

    _____

INDEX